Making Baby Humans

A Single Man's Quest
to Become a Non-traditional Biological Father

Joseph Hahle

CREATESPACE
INDEPENDENT PUBLISHING PLATFORM

MAKING BABY HUMANS
A SINGLE MAN'S QUEST TO BECOME A NON-TRADITIONAL
BIOLOGICAL FATHER

Author: Joseph Hahle

Copy Editor: Lori Bjork http://loribjork.tumblr.com/loris411

Published in the United States by
CreateSpace Independent Publishing Platform

ISBN-10: 154136192X
ISBN-13: 978-1541361928
First Edition: October, 2018

For more information or for updates, please visit:
www.MakingBabyHumans.com

Contents

Introduction

There are more and more people in the world today seeking biological parenthood outside of the traditional process. In the wake of landmark legislation legalizing same sex marriage, many gay couples are looking to expand their families. Others may be straight couples that require the assistance of a surrogate, egg donor, sperm donor, in-vitro fertilization, or any of dozens of procedures needed in order for them to have a biological child of their own. Yet others are singles of either gender seeking their dream of parenthood despite the lack of a permanent romantic partner.

In my case, I'm a single man who utilized an egg donor and surrogate mother in a clinical setting, in a foreign country, to create my biological offspring of a chosen gender. My personal scenario is one of the most complicated ways in the world to go about having a child. Misstep and danger occurred at almost every turn. It never would have happened without sustained, relentless determination fueled by passion in my heart for a child of my own.

As I write this, my twin sons, Alex and Max, are two years old. They're into everything! It's incredible, no matter how well a room is prepared for them, just how fast they can locate something that is dangerous or destructive. Their mission in life seems to be to find the one activity present in a room, which may interfere most with what their caretaker is trying to accomplish, and do it. *And* they are awesome. Their giggles of joy, their fascination with every new thing, the way they light up when you come into a room – it's incomparable. Their presence has expanded my life in ways I could not have imagined. They're typical two-year old boys. They are very healthy, yet just a little smaller than other kids their age due to a significant birth prematurity. As is common with premature children, they've also been delayed in their speech skills. Most kids like them catch up with their size and speech in coming years.

I've pictured that inevitable moment in my head many times when my sons would put two and two together, and start asking questions about where they came from and why they don't have a mother like the other kids do. Every new single or gay parent has envisioned his or her own version of this day. It's dawned on me that no brief explanation could be as meaningful as the full story of their origin. While I won't be asking my toddlers to read a novel, I believe there is no better way for an outside reader to feel the passion inside me for my sons, than to hear the words that I would use to speak to them directly. For this reason I have chosen to tell this story in the form of a letter to Alex and Max. Perhaps they will read this book a number of times throughout their lives as their intellect and experience grows. Perhaps, with each reading, they will gain new insight as to how precious and meaningful their lives are to me and everyone who loves them.

The Big Question

Dear Alex and Max,

You asked me yesterday where your mother is, and I hesitated in my reply. I used to think answering that question would be easy. The intense love in my heart and confidence in my ability to give you a quality home vanquished all doubts from my mind regarding the choices I made. Yet, time has flown by. You're already noticing differences and looking for answers – answers that are easily contemplated, but much harder to actually speak.

The simplest way for me to put this is that I have always been your father *and* mother. And I love you more than you can imagine. Your mother isn't missing. She didn't abandon you. She isn't held against her will in some far away place. She didn't die of an accident or disease or crime. She simply never was.

Technically, there were *two* women who were intimately involved in your beginning. One of them gave a tiny sample of herself, which helps you look the way that you do. The other woman carried you in her tummy until it was time for you to be born. But as precious and generous as they were, neither of them was your mother. *I* am your mother. Your grandmother and grandfather are your mother. All of the women in your life are giving a little more of themselves to help fill that gap. In many ways, you have more mother than many children of the world who were conceived naturally.

It is important for you to know that your lives came about and exist exactly as intended. I believe it is destiny for you to be who you are, and your family to be what it is.

If you still feel short changed, I can understand. There is no one to blame for the circumstances of your creation except me – and God. If it helps, I'm more than willing to say, "I'm sorry." Yet, I would not have done what I did if I did not believe there was more to be gained than lost for you. What I have told you is the truth. Yet, nothing that covers one page can do justice in explaining just how positively miraculous and fantastic the two of you are. So I'm going to start from the beginning. It may be years before you can understand everything I'm about to say, but you'll hear it all. And maybe, in reading, you'll feel something that words alone cannot adequately express. I'm going to tell you the story of how you came to be, and why you're not simply ordinary, but extraordinary.

It was about 1:30AM in Burbank, California. I exited the building I was in and headed down the dark, quiet street on foot. I was working the night shift as a junior editor at a post-production company. It was common for me to step out for a bit around this time of night to stretch my legs.

I was single and, in my opinion, middle-aged. My distinctly calm personality and mild social awkwardness hid my core, which was unexpectedly creative and determined. I'd spent a considerable amount of time seeking a romantic partner with little success. So I had redirected most of my energy outside of my television career towards creative projects.

My house, which I had recently bought, was my pride and joy. It sat comfortably in a modest, middle class neighborhood not far from the freeway, and with a park about a block away down the street. I was fanatical about improvements. My latest innovation was a large, concrete, in-ground spa with waterfall that I built mostly on my own. The house had five bedrooms, and without a family, I was able to rent out four of them for extra cash. My mind was always working on several ways to innovate or build something nobody else ever thought of.

I thought about a lot of different things on those late night walks. But something deep was harassing me that night. I thought to myself, "I'm 36 years old. How is it that I haven't had a child yet? Why do I not have a son or daughter? The best time in life to have a child is say, between 25 and 35 years of age. So where is mine? Ever since I understood the concept as a child that I may one day be a father, I knew I wanted to be one. And I have not made any decisions to the contrary. So…" I couldn't help but wonder, "What the hell happened?!?!" I was obviously pretty frustrated.

The reasons that I had not had a child were quite obvious, actually. I was a gay man who had chosen a career that ended up requiring about a decade to get fully up to speed. No wife, an income that barely paid my own rent, and later a mortgage, for me equaled no children. Add to the mix that I've always been a very responsible person – including in my teens – and even an accidental pregnancy was not going to happen. All the while my desire to be a father, and all that entailed had not changed. As I walked down the street that night, I was aware that, thanks to a career that was finally paying off a bit, I had some money.

Sometimes when I'm making a big decision – particularly if it is about whether or not to experience something – I envision myself on my deathbed. I try to put myself in that perspective and look back at the life I have lived. Then I attempt to judge how I would feel about having experienced or not having experienced something. If I looked back and saw that I had never jumped out of a plane with a parachute, honestly, I don't think I would be disappointed. If I looked back and saw that I had never been to Hawaii, despite that being something that appeals to me, I don't think it would bother me too much. Yet, when I thought about looking back and seeing that I had never been a father, it literally made me want to vomit. Clearly, this was one of the key experiences I wanted to have before my life was through.

I recognized that there were many questions that I needed to answer for myself before moving forward. Was biological parenting the right path for me?

Should I consider adoption? I knew there was a multitude of precious children in the world in need of a quality parent. Depending on what kind of procedures a person required for biological parenting, generally speaking, adopting was a whole lot less expensive.

I had to ask myself, was I really *ready* to have a child of my own? After thinking about this and talking with others, it appeared that few people who have children really know when they're ready, even if they think they know. There are just too many possible variables. An unanticipated illness of a parent or child could pop up and make things difficult. A job could unexpectedly be lost. A romantic relationship could sour. And there are few ways to really know what it's like to be a parent other than experiencing it for yourself. A good friend told me that parents adapt to the situation at hand and make it work – whatever the hardship. I believed this held true for good parents. That isn't to say that anyone should just jump in and hope for the best.

I resolved that a person could address the readiness issue by answering two questions: Question number one: Do I really *want* a child and all of the responsibility involved over the next 20 or more years? We're talking about feeding and diaper changing every 3 hours, daily baths, daily screaming, dressing, teething, messy colds and illnesses, laundry, shopping, furniture, immunization, doctor visits, to and from school a million times, haircuts, lunch pails, school supplies, homework, girlfriends, boyfriends, misbehavior, backtalk, car accidents, tooth cavities, up at night worried, college tuition, and the list could go on and on. Question number two: Do I really have the *financial capacity* to provide a quality life for a child over the next 20 or more years? I had recently heard a statistic that claimed that the average, middle-income cost of raising a child to 19 years of age in the United States was $240,000. That's an average of $1,053 per month for 19 years! I mulled the above questions and felt strongly that my answer to both was "yes."

I considered how many children were born to parents who weren't even really thinking about parenthood. Some precious children were conceived accidentally by parents who didn't even know each other before they had too many drinks one night at a bar. I was serious about being a parent. I felt that my deliberateness was the first thing that qualified me to be a parent.

I knew that I would be sentencing you to a life without a traditional mother. Regardless, I was convinced that a child did not require two traditional parents to have a quality upbringing. After a child's basic needs are met, the key to successful parenting is loving a child unconditionally. My child would have multiple other strong female figures in his or her life to help fill that void.

Another consideration to be made when deciding whether or not to become a non-traditional biological parent was how the circumstances of the child's origin might affect him or her. I knew that someday you would have to be informed that I was gay and you were created in a laboratory with no mother. You would naturally compare your circumstances with that of your peers and realize that you were different. At the same time, your peers presumably would know this information and could use it to harass you. The truth is, all of this ran through my head early on, but did not stick. As far as I was concerned, none of these things had any bearing on the value or quality of a person whatsoever. Any repercussions were only possibilities, not inevitabilities. In that conversation when I would explain to you how you came to be, I would quickly remind you how every child is different. Some have no father, others have no grandparents. Some are born with a physical or mental handicap, others are adopted. Some kids are rich, while starved of personal attention from their parents. Some kids have a seemingly perfect life, only to die in a tragic accident before they become adults. I recognize these are graphic, depressing examples for a young child. You get my point. All of these kids would be precious and priceless, each with their own circumstances including advantages and disadvantages.

You had the potential of being fully healthy. You would grow up in a loving and stable home with a dedicated father, a close relationship with two exceptional grandparents, in a nice house, with two sets of aunts and uncles, and five cousins. You would have a treasure trove of blessings and quality role models. Heck, any more advantages and your life might be almost... boring. Yes, you would have to ward off potential heckling from your classmates. Yet, if every child with a disadvantage had parents who saw that as a reason to not have children, I dare say the schools would be empty.

I never ruled out adoption, but decided that I would prefer having a biological child. My reasons for this had more to do with instinct than a calculation. Beyond that, I was aware that my particular clan of Hahles in the United States was without a male heir. We had all descended from my great-Grandfather, Carl Hahle, who had emigrated from Germany in 1884 when he was only 10. With all of the other males in the family considerably older, years ago having concluded their expected childbearing possibilities, our Hahle name, by blood, would likely disappear if I did not have a son.

In the end, I decided not to feel judged for my choice. I knew that hundreds of thousands of babies are born every day to their biological parents. Most of those parents didn't question their right to have such a child. Neither would I.

Ever heard of kids in their teens who make agreements that if they are not married by a certain age, they will marry each other? I had made an agreement with myself some years earlier that my deadline for becoming a parent was 40 years of age. I wasn't quite sure how I would deal with that when the time came, but the clock was ticking. As I continued to walk down those dark streets in Burbank every work night, I had the distinct and ominous feeling that my time was running out. I noticed children everywhere with their parents: at the park, in the mall, at church, in restaurants and walking down the sidewalk past my house. Everywhere! Where was mine?!? I had to make this happen. I had to gather my resources, do the work involved, and make this happen. *Now.*

I was in the final stages of deciding to go all out to become a biological father when I started sharing my plans with a few people around me. I was amazed at how many friends were willing to express directly to my face that they felt it was wrong for a single person to have their own biological child. There was one particular friend I debated with quite a lot. In one specific discussion I said to him, "So what about single people who have children accidentally and who are entirely unprepared?"

He replied, "It was an accident. There's nothing that can be done about that."

I replied, "So they are allowed. But I, someone who actually wants a child and is prepared to provide for a child, am not allowed?"

He responded with a self-satisfied nod, "It is your conscious intention to be a father that disqualifies you from having a child accidentally."

I recognized that his answer and general argument was technically logical. In my heart, my enthusiasm for the idea of parenting overrode the sentiment I was getting from him and others, which was so cold and clinical.

After thinking for a while, I realized that everyone who was giving me negative feedback was someone who didn't have children, and really didn't want children for themselves – no matter what the circumstance. Not everyone was so negative. My parents were quite supportive. A few other close friends loved the idea and even wanted to be involved.

I remember one of my close friends telling me, "Joe, you've got such an even, calm demeanor. I imagine that would be extremely comforting for a young child."

Another friend said, "Joe, plant your garden early. Harvest is years away. You need to be able to run and jump the whole way through."

Another friend was looking straight into my eyes across a

restaurant dinner table. "Joe," he stated intently. "If you really want to do this," pausing for effect, "You need to do it NOW."

Over the next several months, I was saving up every dime I could.

Joseph Hahle, Hollywood, CA, 2012.

Choosing a Method
of Baby-Making

Decision time! I had decided to become a non-traditional
biological parent – or at least give it a shot. Now I had to decide
how I wanted to go about it.

My research showed me that if you are a single woman with
good reproductive health, it should be fairly easy to use a sperm
bank utilizing frozen sperm, or have someone you know donate
sperm. The woman would collect and utilize the specimen
according to her fertility doctor's instructions. She would use a
legal contract to define rights to the offspring – either through
the sperm bank or independently. At the time, the law favored
(and most likely still does) biological mothers. Assuming she has
the ability to care for the child, she would not have any issues
maintaining legal custody. This type of person had the easiest
option for becoming a non-traditional biological parent.

For men it was a whole different ballgame! And there were a
number of options.

Option 1: I could simply copulate with a friend or other
chosen casual partner. If actual copulation was undesired, my
semen could be deposited into a cup. Then a turkey baster-like
device could be used by the female to insert the fluid. This
method would need to be repeated until success was achieved.
This method is very similar to traditional biological parenting,
but still qualified as non-traditional, because I would still be
asking my friend to be a surrogate. An agreement would be

made regarding compensation to the surrogate, and my custody of a resulting child could range from 0 to 100%. This might have been the least expensive and least complicated option – up front.

Yet, there are enormous risks. If a child was conceived, once it was born, the birth mother may have second thoughts about giving up her rights to the baby. Because the child would be her genetic offspring, if she wanted to keep it, it very well may end up with her – even if she and I had both signed a contract stating otherwise. This would be especially true if the surrogate was coupled or married. Also, in the case of a birth mother who decides to keep her baby, despite not having custody of the child, I might still be liable for child support. I was also likely to have to pay for all of the mother's medical care during the pregnancy and birth. So if my goal was a child that lived with me, I felt this avenue was a non-starter.

It may have been easier said than done anyway. I've heard plenty of guys say they have a female friend who is just waiting for the chance to be their surrogate. I believe this is an easy offer to make, but a very difficult action to follow through with – if their plan is to actually give up the child.

Option 2: The pregnancy would be achieved in a clinical setting using deposited semen and eggs. In my case, the semen would be from me and the eggs would be from the surrogate. This option was largely no longer permitted because the baby to be born would be the surrogate's genetic offspring. The genetic connection would make it much more likely for the surrogate to change her mind about giving up the baby, and would make it that much more likely that she would win custody in such an event.

Option 3: As a single man, wanting a child that was biologically mine, and with my custody guaranteed, I would require an egg donor with separate surrogate carrier. In this situation, the resulting child would have no genetic connection to the surrogate, keeping the lines much more clearly defined regarding rights. This was the most complicated and most expensive option. And, I decided it was the right option for me.

Frustratingly, nailing down that huge expense was elusive. I wasn't ready to talk to fertility clinics, so all of my learning was still happening online. What *was* becoming clear, the costs were unpredictable. No website could specify for sure how much it would cost me, because there were too many variables. Almost all of the steps along the way came with a price. Any of these steps might need to be repeated many times until success was achieved – if it ever was. Unless a clinic was offering a special guarantee that one price would pay for unlimited procedure attempts, the costs for achieving a birth appeared potentially limitless.

I set a goal for myself to have $70,000 in hand before taking serious action. This was a big figure for me – twice the down payment for my house, which had taken me years to accumulate. With luck, I just might have that amount of money by October.

Choosing an Egg/Sperm Donor

October arrived. I was on schedule with my savings. So it was time to make things happen. After money, the next thing on my mind was who the other half of the genetic material would come from – who the egg donor would be.

Max and Alex, when you look at your hand and notice how it's shaped, look into a mirror and recognize yourself, or interact with someone and sense your own personality traits, you're experiencing samples of who you are. Max, you seem to be obsessed with how objects connect and disconnect. And you have such a strong voice that, when you want to, you can make my ears ring even when you're 20 feet away. Alex, you are so in love with trains and planes. And when you figure out that you like something, getting and holding that particular thing is all you care about in the world. You're both very physically affectionate. A lot of who you are is determined by your own completely unique blend of genes – the "blueprints" that determine your design. You have a set of these in every single cell in your bodies. No one else that ever existed has the same set.

Just the timing involved in which sperm cell would fertilize your egg has been influenced by nearly infinite events in distant corners of the universe since the beginning of time itself. The chances of you turning out just the way you are, are incalculable. Always remember that no matter what your genes determine about you, many of the things in you, that are the most important, come from what you choose. Also know that while half of your genes come from me, the other half of your genes come from someone very special, whom I chose with great care.

When traditional couples initially fall in love, they generally aren't giving any conscious thought to who the other genetic parent of their children will be. When they produce a child, there is no choice in this matter. It's all lined up. The other genetic parent is their romantic partner. I suppose from a scientific perspective, they are making that choice, perhaps subconsciously, when they choose their romantic partner to begin with.

Yet honestly, I think few of these couples are consciously looking over their partner's attributes, contemplating whether or not they want their child to have that curly hair, or those eyes, height, nose, or intellect. Yet when you're choosing an egg or sperm donor specifically to be the biological parent of your future child, and with so many options, suddenly this can become quite a daunting decision! Now, for the record, I knew there were people who intentionally chose their donor anonymously – meaning they went to a donor agency and had the choice made at random – with no knowledge of any of the characteristics of the donor whatsoever. I suppose that is really quite altruistic. After all, any child, regardless of his or her attributes is just as valid and worthy of life and love as any other. This method ensures the parent steers entirely clear of any form of prejudice. Yet, many of us can't possibly ignore the opportunity to make an informed decision. After all, traditional parents do choose, whether consciously or unconsciously, whom they want for their romantic partner. It isn't random.

If you were a baby, not yet conceived, destined to come into the world, wouldn't you want your parent/parents to make the best decision they could regarding who would contribute half of your genes, rather than being acquired at random? I respect everyone's choice in how they handle this decision. For me, a most careful and deliberate choice it had to be.

I had thought about all the women that I knew personally, and whether or not I would consider asking any of them for their eggs. Knowing the egg donor personally might be important to some people. In my case, I really didn't want any long-term connection with the egg donor. I didn't want any future complications regarding who your parent was. Also, it was important to me that I receive a thorough list of the egg donor's personal and family history, especially regarding health. Can you imagine how awkward it would be to get approval from someone you knew personally to use their eggs, only to reject them later on after learning about some bit of family history that you never knew about? As it turned out, all of the women I knew just didn't work for me for one reason or another, anyway.

So I turned back to the internet. This led me to various U.S. egg donor agencies. These agencies had hundreds of donors for me to choose from. The cost of one batch of donor eggs through a U.S. agency ranged between five and ten thousand dollars. Each donor came with a long list of traits and other information. I started reviewing and comparing potential donors immediately, sensing that this search could become quite involved.

I saw two sets of criteria available to choose an egg donor. One set of information was about characteristics that could not be seen, such as intelligence, personality type, and health history of the donor and their family. In the case of intelligence, this was a bit hard to nail down. Most of what was listed had to do with how far a donor went with school, which may or may not have a correlation with her genetic imprinting. My aunt suggested to me that personality type was the most important characteristic. Great suggestion, yet honestly, could you imagine an egg donor advertising anything other than positive personality traits? They weren't going to mention a short temper or that they were constantly contrary. I'm not saying the search was hopeless. I'm just saying it was complicated.

Then there were the characteristics that *could* be seen, including "looks." Some intended parents want a donor who looks just like them. I suppose, with a donor absent as a child is growing up, that would make it a little easier to pretend that the donor never existed, and the child came entirely from the intended parent, thereby reducing the sense that something is missing. Others prefer a donor who would add to and enhance their own genetic makeup. I probably belonged in this grouping. One thing I had hoped you would inherit from an egg donor was an enhanced ability to tan in the sun, or withstand the sun's rays. After 20 minutes of direct exposure to mid-day summer sun, my skin starts to burn. An inheritance of more resilient (darker) skin pigment would benefit you throughout your life. In addition, I simply admire the look of less pale skin.

It was extremely important for me to keep in mind that when choosing an egg donor, essentially no genetic traits found in the donor were guaranteed to materialize in you. The nature of conception was a random combining of genetic information from chromosomes that could not be predicted. A gene governing eye color could come from the mother, while a gene determining mental creativity could come from the father. Also, we all carry lots of genes that are dormant. A particular nose shape may not have been seen in the family for two generations. A mother and father with dark brown hair may have a baby with the most striking red hair, and so on. The specific outcomes, with very few exceptions, were not guaranteed. That doesn't stop would-be parents from trying to stack the deck to favor one trait or another.

On television, I had seen composite (blended) images of a mother and father that attempted to predict the appearance of their future child. I figured this was highly inexact. However, I must admit that I did use this technique on a number of occasions to get a rough idea of potential results, as well as simply out of extreme curiosity. One easy and free website for facial compositing was www.morphthing.com.

There were all sorts of women to choose from at the agency websites. Traits included most anything one could think of, such as: red hair, green eyes, tall, short, long-lived family, artistic, bubbly personality, and multiple higher education degrees. These were just a few of the types of attributes one would read. Photographs accompanied most donor profiles. Some had donated before, and would list the number of eggs harvested and number of pregnancies that had resulted. One agency would only display photographs of the donors as children. Another agency was highly exclusive – displaying only women with higher education degrees and model-like appearance, as well as a considerably "enhanced" price tag. Though I respected each of these groups for whatever their philosophy, I couldn't help feel that the exclusive one was selling egg donors who used a lot of makeup, were on intense diets, and came from well privileged families that could afford all that college education – attributes that had very little to do with genes. Generally, egg donors were preferred to be in their 20's, and most donors in the agencies seemed to be. My understanding was that the likelihood of eggs resulting in successful pregnancies went down considerably each year after age 30 for the donor.

At first, it might sound like, with all of these options, how could one fail to find just the right donor? I soon learned that there was even more complication than was first apparent. Some donors specified that they would only donate to couples. A few even specified they would only donate to a couple of a particular religion. I also found quickly than no matter how many profiles I reviewed, none displayed information that matched my ideal donor list – the contents of which I consider private. This should not have come as a surprise to me. My list was long, and I know all people are unique. We all have flaws and combinations of so many characteristics. Please do not misunderstand. I was not determined to design the perfect baby. There is no such thing. I was simply trying to make the best decision that I possibly could.

Over a number of days of looking, I adjusted my attitude to allow for some flexibility and did eventually find a donor profile that satisfied me. In fact, I was quite excited. She was Puerto Rican, with the most amazing smile, a zeal for health and fitness, a good education, and a self-professed desire to help someone who wanted to be a parent, amongst many other qualities that I really liked. This girl was *not* perfect or a super model. Yet, there was something about her that drew me in. In finding her, I realized that this whole process was not going to be strictly scientific. Just like the ordinary person who met someone interesting and ended up falling in love, I spotted this girl, found myself mysteriously attracted, and therefore willing. It wasn't that her personal information lined up just right with my list. It just *felt* right.

I needed to get some other things in line before moving forward. Yet just maybe, this was a big part of the puzzle that I had already figured out! Time would tell.

Choosing a Fertility Clinic

Making phone calls to do research or find someone who can provide a particular service was not my favorite thing. I knew that at some point early in this process, I would need to talk to and work with real experts who could help me achieve a pregnancy. Basically, I needed a fertility specialist and clinic. Everyone has heard of a fertility clinic. Making a baby in an unconventional way, I was going to get up close and personal, and I was going to become quite familiar with what these facilities really do.

I picked up my phone and started calling the local clinics. In Los Angeles there were quite a few. My intension was to get some price quotes and set up an interview with two or three clinics that felt right. A middle aged sounding woman answered the first call.

"West Coast Fertility, may I help you?"

"Yes," I answered. "My name is Joe. I'm interested in your IVF services."

"Oh, very good. We're happy to assist you. And what is your wife's name?"

"I don't have a wife. I'm single."

"Oh... I'm sorry. We only provide services for women and couples."

"Oh... Ok. Well, thank you anyway." I hung up the phone and called the next clinic.

"Hello?" the receptionist asked.

"Hi. My name is Joe. I'm interested in your IVF services."

"Oh. What would you like to know?"

"Can you give me an estimate of the expenses involved?"

"You'll have to make an appointment to come in and see the doctor with your wife."

"Actually, I'm not married."

"Oh... well, you can bring in your girlfriend. That's fine."

"No, no. I'm single. I don't have a girlfriend."

"Oh," long pause, "what's the procedure for then?"

"I plan to use an egg donor and surrogate to carry the child."

"Oh... I'm sorry; I don't think we do that unless your wife is present."

I made yet another call with a similar outcome. I was more than a little surprised and disillusioned. This was certainly not the first time an unmarried man sought professional services to make himself a father. We've all heard stories about single celebrities, and a few of us average folks, having their own children using egg donors, IVF, and surrogacy. Yet I couldn't get past a short phone conversation. And I hadn't even mentioned yet that I was gay! This wasn't the law getting in the way. This was independent clinics writing their own narrow-minded policy which stated that I was simply not qualified to participate in their programs. And this wasn't a smaller, conservative town in the Midwest. This was the modern, liberal, diverse, international, well-gay-populated, city of Los Angeles, California!

I thought to myself, "For the first time in human history, the knowledge and technology is present and legal to make someone like me a biological father. I *may* even have the required money. But, they just won't. Perfect."

I pressed on with my calls, and eventually discovered there were a rare few clinics that would work with single men. As soon as I found someone who said "yes," I also started getting some real answers regarding cost. I was quite unimpressed. Although the numbers could not be guaranteed, the clinics I had spoken with were giving me good reason to believe that, up to a birth, I was likely to spend $120,000 or more. That was $50,000 more than I had saved, and was just an estimated starting price!

Again, I was discouraged. My research into the cost of egg donation, IVF and surrogacy in the U.S. was resulting in numbers that were, frankly, unrealistic for me. Maybe this dream really was honestly out of my grasp. Thoughts crept into my mind of starting to research the local adoption agencies. I moped around not feeling right about much of anything.

"There must be a way," I thought to myself. "There must be something I haven't considered."

Within days, I was researching clinics outside of the United States. I had already heard that people were traveling abroad for all sorts of medical care due to unaffordable costs here, which is referred to as medical tourism. From hip replacements, to dental procedures, to face lifts, choose the appropriate foreign destination, and almost any medical service can be performed by a true expert with state-of-the art technology at a fraction of the cost found in the U.S., and that apparently included IVF and surrogacy. Rumor had it that India was an especially popular place to go, so I started running internet searches. As soon as you start looking abroad for this kind of service, you notice that each country has its list of restrictions on what you can and cannot do legally. For instance, in one country, single would-be parents may be banned from all services. In another country, surrogacy may be allowed, but only by a member of your existing family. Such was the case in Brazil at the time. In another country, a specific procedure, such as PGD (Pre-implantation genetic diagnosis) may be banned. And it appeared like the laws were changing from year to year.

I began to fear the possibility that I would find a clinic in another country that was willing to work with someone like me, had rates that I could actually afford, yet would be unable to proceed due to law. Such was the case in India. I wanted to use PGD for gender selection. At that time, that procedure was not allowed by law for ethical reasons. While still researching India, I happened across a website for a particular international clinic called, *New Life*, with offices in a number of countries. The site led me to their branch in Bangkok, Thailand, where all of the services I required were permitted. Their breakdown of costs suggested a price tag of around $40,000 if all went well. That was one *third* the estimate I had received in America!

My research of IVF opportunities internationally did not initially end when I discovered the New Life clinic in Bangkok. I'm someone who likes to know all of the options available before making a choice. Yet as I made my way around to various countries, I found that each had something that wasn't quite right for me. As I corresponded with the Thai clinic, the representative there made me feel like I was completely welcome. I was impressed by what I was learning about their technical knowledge and facilities, which seemed entirely state of the art. It became more and more clear that this was the company with which I would go through this journey. With options worldwide, it was a great relief to finally be able to focus on one place and facility. It felt like I was about to really get something done.

Talking to My Parents

It was probably a full year, or even two, before my search for a clinic, that I began talking with your Grandma and Grandpa about my hopes to become a father. My parents are amazing people. My father, now retired, is an ordained Lutheran pastor. He and my mother were married shortly before embarking on what would be 12 years as Christian missionaries in the mid 60's – 70's in the small country of Guyana, South America. They spent a good chunk of that time living on a river with no roads in a remote area of the rainforest. It takes a special breed to do that successfully, and my parents did it with conviction. They returned to America with three sons, me being the youngest, and my father went on to lead successful ministries for another 30 years until his retirement.

So, ever since I can remember, Dad was always the leader of a church. He wore a fancy robe, preached the sermon, and sat in the most conspicuous chair. From a child's perspective, this could look like a throne. And the church has always been the center of our lives. I say this to illustrate how big my dad is in our family. Growing up, he was not only the leader of the church, but also the wisest and most naturally respected man I knew. There were plenty of debates in our house, as in any, but when my dad gave an order, no-one questioned him. All of this might sound like someone who was egotistical and authoritarian, but nothing could be further from the truth. Dad was considerate and patient, soft-spoken, modest, gentle, always looking for consensus and reconciliation. It's hard to understand how that personality type could yield near total subordination from us kids from our toddler stage all the way through early adulthood, but it did! He's not a perfect man, by any means. Yet my dad resembles Christ more than any person I have ever known. Of course, this just adds to his esteem.

It has been said that behind every great man is a great woman. This would surely be the case here. My mom is my dad's opposite in many ways. What he lacks in emotional expression, she more than makes up for. She can be very spontaneous and extroverted. Her love for her family is equaled only by her conviction to what *she feels* is right. My mother is also known in the family for a streak of what I will call "eccentricity". This has many manifestations. One that comes to mind is her insistence that the house must be cleaned and trash removed immediately before a trip. I cannot recall how many times the family has sat grumbling in the car, behind schedule, for a long awaited trip departure, while my mom vacuumed the carpets in the house.

My mother's peculiarities are often harnessed to a more worthy cause. I like to tell a story of one morning when she was driving me to school in the 7th grade. We were running late and had made it about a block from home. She asked me if I had brushed my teeth. Sensing the futility of the question at this point, I uttered the truth, "No, I didn't have time." The brakes were quickly applied and, to my amazement and frustration, we immediately returned to the house so I could brush my teeth. I didn't even have any cavities. For a 13 year old, I did a pretty great job with my teeth. I don't know why I was surprised that she turned around. Mom was always doing radical things like that. I think it was her way of emphasizing the importance of the principals she held most dear. At the moment of an incident, her actions were usually quite annoying. Yet, as I grew up, I occasionally really admired her ability to stand out and do ridiculous things for the causes she believed in.

Another incident that comes to mind involved an 8th grade social studies teacher that was giving me a hard time. This guy was a real jerk. Every day in class he would do something to demean or humiliate a student. It wasn't in humor. He was just a cranky, bitter, scrawny bully. He gave me my fair share of grief, which I told my mom about. At the impending parent/teacher conference, you might have thought she would give him a taste of his own medicine. You would be wrong. Instead, she pulled him aside and impressed upon him that she and my dad were very happy he was my teacher! She said that he starred at her like antennas were growing out of her head. I wasn't pleased, at first, that she had been nice to him. Yet, after the conference, that teacher never gave me a hard time again. I learned something about going against the grain to make a positive impact on someone.

Needless to say, your grandparents loom large in my life. Today, I'm a very independent adult who has been responsible for his own matters for quite a long time, and I've done plenty of things that my parents did not prescribe. There have been sections of my adult life that have passed when my parents lived in another part of the country, and I could not expect to see them more than once or twice during the course of a year. I've never been a big phone talker with anybody. So, sometimes weeks would pass during which I would have no contact with my parents at all.

That said, over the years, and more and more recently, there have been various moments that have revealed to me just how much I still depend on my parents to define my very life. I truly believe that at the end of the day, most of what I do, consciously or unconsciously, I do to make my parents proud. When the mythical day comes when I have reached the height of my accomplishments in this world, I will undoubtedly look to my parents for approval. They may or may not be particularly impressed. For me, their witness of my life somehow makes it valid. I'm well aware that when that day comes, one or both of them may not be present to respond. I may someday need to re-evaluate what I see as my purpose in life. Just maybe, that purpose will be redirected to someone who is dependent on me, rather than I on them.

My description of how important Christianity is in our family might make one expect that my coming out as a gay person, or wanting to become a father as a single gay man, would be met with strong disapproval. You cannot get a clear sense of who my parents are without knowing that they are both open minded people, who put their unconditional love of their children and the quest for sensible answers to life's difficult questions above any tradition. When I came out as a gay person, despite not having any experience with gay people, my parents embraced my orientation and came to a new understanding. They have stood in support of gay rights ever since.

As I talked with my parents about my fathering ambitions, even from the beginning, I was talking mostly about biological parenting, but also a bit about adoption. Both of them were supportive. I remember my dad being particularly encouraging. I suspect he saw me as someone who would make a very good parent, and who should make an attempt soon before I was too old. He possibly also liked the idea that I might provide a grandson. My older brothers were finished having children and had provided 5 granddaughters.

Despite this apparent support, I found on a number of occasions, when I would talk about all the research and progress I was making, that my parents would respond with a hesitant "hmm," or "okay," and then change the subject or tell me it was a long day and they were off to bed. I wasn't sure what to make of this. Below is an excerpt from actual email correspondence between my parents and me. I sent the message to them after I reported on one of the egg donor candidates, sending a photograph. They seemed like they barely noticed.

"Dear Mom and Dad,

...I'm doing the best job I know how to do with this. I've saved up the money and made a decision to give it a try. If I fail, I'll simply pursue other options towards fatherhood. The path forward over the coming 18 to 24 months is full of hurdles and uncertainty. It's not the sort of thing that one broadcasts to the world. So I need both of you to be on board! Please be engaged. Ask questions. Celebrate with me when something goes right. And give me some encouragement when challenges arise.

Love,
Joe"

My mom replied quickly,

"Hi Joe!

Great pictures! We were delighted to see them! I think you made a good choice. We certainly hope all goes well as you proceed.

How did you learn about the agency you are working with? You want to know that they are dependable and that you can trust them. You will want them to work with you to ensure that an egg or eggs are donated and sent and arrive where you expect them. Keep us posted.

There are always concerns and questions and risks with having a child. But, having a child can be one of the greatest joys of life.

We pray for the best.
Love,
Mom"

The reply I received made me feel much better, and was the beginning of a much more healthy communication between us from that point forward.

Choosing an Egg Donor
Part II

I felt good about finding a clinic that I could bond with. Now, all I had to do was coordinate the clinic with my chosen egg donor, the Puerto Rican girl with the great smile! She would need to travel to Thailand for the egg retrieval procedure. The clinic in Bangkok was happy to do this.

But, reading the fine print at the egg donor agency website, I discovered a serious problem. The agency in the U.S., which happened to be in Atlanta, would not allow its donors to travel internationally.

"You've got to be kidding me!" I thought. "Another unnecessary road block!"

With just a little more research, I discovered this was standard U.S. egg donor agency policy. I considered the idea of contacting my chosen egg donor privately to arrange the travel and procedure without the agency involved. Yet U.S. egg donor agencies were also extremely careful about protecting the identity of their donors. I didn't have a name. All I had was a few photographs and a list of characteristics and statistics. I didn't even know for certain which city she lived in. So this did not seem practical.

What made more sense to me was the idea of egg freezing. I could have the egg retrieval procedure done in Atlanta where the eggs would be frozen and sent to the clinic in Thailand. My research showed me that egg freezing and transporting was being done more and more. So I set out to call the fertility clinics in Atlanta to arrange the retrieval, freezing and transporting of the eggs to Thailand.

Two days later, after making at least 20 calls, I was again abruptly thwarted. Despite the fact that the egg freezing and transporting technology was proven and available, not a single one of the clinics I located would allow the release of frozen eggs off their premises, simply due to their own independent policy. I'm not sure if they feared liability, or if they just wanted to guarantee that any procedures to follow were done in their clinic where they would profit. Either way, getting my chosen egg donor's – or *any* U.S. agency egg donor's – eggs to my clinic in Thailand seemed impossible. So I was forced to give up on any of those donors, including the Puerto Rican girl I had been so pleased to find!!

I was becoming very accustomed to hearing the word "no." I could just see myself in a giant maze. The egg donor I had my heart set on was in plain view just ahead. While in reaching for her hand, my face met abruptly with a stiff pane of glass, sealing her out of reach. I was running into this sort of dead end at almost every turn. Thankfully, up to that point, perseverance always revealed some new path forward. But would the path ever lead to you? I did not know.

The hunt for a brand new egg donor was on. Where would I find her? I discovered that my clinic in Thailand had its own database of egg donors from both Southeast Asia and various parts of the Eastern hemisphere. Their database was much smaller than that of the U.S. agencies, and at first look, I wasn't satisfied.

I searched the globe with an international website that reminded me of a dating website. Most of the donors there were beyond the ideal age range and expressed restriction for those who were not straight couples. I even posted some ads on

Craigslist, and received a few, very-sincere-sounding replies from women who were interested, along with a few messages that were not tasteful or encouraging at all. No one I was coming in contact with seemed like "the one." Besides that, the donors at the official agencies had been vetted. They had all been through counseling and some form of screening for genetic and mental health. If I found a girl on my own, I'd have to arrange all of that myself, or take some pretty big risks with a stranger.

A new possibility in America surfaced. There was a facility in Phoenix, Arizona called The World Egg Bank. This place sounded entirely different. Unlike typical fertility clinics I had spoken to, who wanted patients who would carry out all of their procedures under one roof, the primary service of The World Egg Bank was to store frozen eggs from its donors, making them available to ship out upon purchase – *international* shipments included. It sounded very similar to a sperm bank. The World Egg Bank was the only place around I had discovered that did this with eggs.

I found a donor in this company's database that did seem like a good fit. Yet there were a couple other considerations that ultimately led to my choice not to take this path. First and foremost was egg count, which my research showed had deep influence on the odds of ultimate success. There was a fair, and significant, charge for the first five eggs purchased. Individual eggs could be purchased after that. The cost added up fast, and there was no way to know if those eggs would ever be needed. Besides that, although The World Egg Bank spoke very confidently about its frozen eggs, its practices were still quite uncommon. Conventionally, it was thought that the odds of successful fertilization were improved with fresh (never frozen) eggs. So after considerable debate, I opted to put The World Egg Bank on standby.

It was weeks later when I went back to the Thai clinic's own database. After reviewing all of the donors present, I reconsidered someone I had noticed before, but passed by a little too quickly. This girl had lots of great statistics. The physical feature that stood out the most was that she was tall and very slim. The composite images (not that they matter) looked really nice. I soon found myself bonding with the idea of this person as my donor. I waited a week; just to be sure I was sure. Then I made the call to lock her in.

Very few calls I had made to this point had resulted in positive results. I had been turned away by numerous clinics due to my personal circumstances. Other clinics gave me the bad news that their services were far out of my budget. Yet other clinics refused to participate in specific procedures that I required. And the egg donor agencies wouldn't let their donors travel out of the country. This next call would be no different. The girl I had chosen was already in the process of donating for someone else. So if I wanted her, and I did, I would have to wait two months. Two months passed and I eagerly checked in to secure the donor. This time I was told the donor had decided to take a break from donating. Indefinitely!

You might think that this would have been a good time for me to give up my quest. Nothing seemed to be working out! Another person may have figured that all of the roadblocks were a sign that this type of parenthood was simply not meant to be for them. Few of my accomplishments in life have been easy. I've always been someone that had to make something happen if I wanted it to. In such a case, I'd say that if God gave me the tools to overcome the obstacles that it *was* meant to be! And I think my attitude about who would make a suitable egg donor for me was continuing to soften, which was probably a healthy thing.

I poured back through the Thai clinic database and came upon a profile that had been there the whole time. This girl lived in South Africa. She was very sweet looking with dark flowing black hair and green eyes. On the less-positive side, her statistics showed that her family was not very tall or long-lived. As I've stated before, humans are mixtures of so many qualities. Her prior donations had yielded a solid 12+ eggs on the average and two pregnancies had resulted – an excellent sign. I did the image compositing that I've spoken of before. Though I maintain that these images have questionable value, some of the pictures were astoundingly good – the best I had seen to that point.

I did my customary waiting and thinking. Then I made the call. This donor, Roxanne, was willing and available! Arrangements were made and a date was set for the egg retrieval, which would be several weeks away. I was so thankful and excited, at long last, to be beyond this hurdle with a choice I felt very good about. For the first time, real action was being taken to create you.

Max and Alex, this compassionate woman, Roxanne, is your biological mother. Later, she was presented the opportunity to meet with us personally, but declined. It is hard to say, but there is a good chance that she felt that not having personal contact with us would make the arrangement less emotionally complicated for her – a sentiment that I could very much understand. There is every reason to believe she is loving and thoughtful, and would have wanted you both to have everything in life. To this day, I am absolutely delighted that she is your biological mother. The information gathered about her prior donations suggests strongly that you have at least two half siblings out there in the world somewhere. Someday, when you are of age, you may choose to do some investigation work to try to find them – if only out of curiosity. Of course, that choice will be yours alone.

Up to this point, everything was hypothetical and without risk. Suddenly, that rocket that had been sitting idle on the pad for months, anticipating a launch, had lifted off and was headed for space. It was at this time I started sending payments to the clinic in Bangkok. I considered making a trip to Thailand personally to confirm authenticity of the company and to leave a sperm sample before making a commitment. Correspondence with the clinic, including references they had provided me, convinced me to proceed without that trip. From that point forward, every few weeks, as things were being accomplished, I was making payments in the thousands of dollars. Each time I wired money, I wondered if this would pay off, or if that money was simply disappearing, never to be seen again.

In-vitro Fertilization

During this wait for the egg retrieval, I continued my research into the details of the laboratory process that resulted in pregnancy. I believed anyone going through this process should have a basic understanding of what was happening under the microscope. I imagine you are curious about how your pregnancy was accomplished.

Most adults have a reasonably good knowledge of how traditional biological reproduction occurs. After the copulation of a male and female, a single sperm cell unites with an egg cell inside the mother. Their DNA strands unravel and combine with each other to form one completely unique set of chromosomes – all of the information needed to make a human being. This cell begins to divide rapidly, forming an embryo, which attaches to the inside of the mother's uterus. After nine months of growth and development, a baby is ready to be born.

All of the same basic steps take place in the laboratory scenario, although, it obviously doesn't start with copulation. The early steps take place in a petri dish rather than a mother's body.

First, egg and sperm cells must be aquired. The sperm cell acquisition is comparatively very easy. The male providing the sperm visits the lab, where a semen specimen is collected in a plastic cup. The sperm material can be utilized fresh within a number of hours or cryogenically frozen in a very particular manner for use weeks, months or even years later.

The acquisition of egg cells is much more complicated, and is done at some risk for the donor. A female's ovaries already contain all of the eggs she will ever have when she is born. Her eggs must develop and mature before they can be used for reproduction, which normally happens very slowly (about once a month) over the course of many years. To acquire enough eggs to be useful in the IVF process, the female will receive certain fertility drugs, over a period of weeks, which help her body mature more eggs at one time than it usually would. In a highly specialized clinical setting, after a specific period of time, the well-developed eggs are collected. There is no guarantee how many eggs will develop adequately. A typical collection could result in between 3 and 20 eggs, but could be considerably more or zero. The number of eggs retrieved can be extremely important, as I will discuss shortly. Freshly collected egg cells are generally used within hours of the retrieval. It is possible to freeze them for much later use – a practice that is becoming more common.

The next step is IVF or in-vitro fertilization – the uniting of sperm and egg. First, the sperm has to be prepared. A typical sample of semen contains 180 million sperm cells, or more, along with a lot of lubricating fluid. All of that has to be sorted out a bit. From millions, a lucky one or more sperm are chosen.

The IVF is then often accomplished using a technique called ICSI or intra-cytoplasmic sperm injection. A single chosen sperm is injected directly into the egg cell. DNA combining will proceed spontaneously and the cell will divide, indicating a successful fertilization. Once each egg has divided into 2 or more cells, it is considered an embryo. This process is completed with all of the egg cells available. Within a few days, each embryo will grow until it contains around 8 cells.

When the doctor is satisfied with the development of the embryos, it is time to conduct the first transfer. The transfer procedure involves inserting embryos into the surrogate mother's uterus. The surrogate mother, who carries the baby to term, is usually a different person than the egg donor, unless she is a woman who is providing eggs and carrying the child for herself. In order to create a pregnancy, the embryos must self-attach to the inner wall of the uterus. Keep in mind that the embryos are microscopic. So once they have been transferred to the surrogate, it's up to nature to take its course. The embryos are gone, or lost, unless they successfully attach and a pregnancy occurs.

The odds of successful embryo attachment inside the uterus are hard to define, but they can be very low – perhaps 10-20%. This is why it is not uncommon for more than one embryo to be used in this expensive, delicate and complex procedure. Transferring two embryos simultaneously increases the likelihood of a pregnancy. It also increases the odds of a fraternal twin pregnancy, if both embryos happen to attach. Certain medications used in fertility treatments increase the likelihood of embryo division, and thus identical twin pregnancies. This is why it is very uncommon, and possibly illegal, for more than three embryos to be transferred. If each of three embryos divides just once and attaches, a single pregnancy of six or more fetuses could easily occur, creating great danger for all involved. Also, caring for the resulting children would be a logistical crisis, should they all be born.

Within days after the transfer, a chemical test can reveal whether or not a pregnancy has occurred.

The process involves many steps. Each step is a hurdle that must be overcome by each egg or embryo. Each time an egg or embryo fails to succeed at a certain step, the number of viable eggs or embryos that one possesses is reduced. So the number of quality eggs that are acquired during the initial egg retrieval is vital. For example, imagine the egg retrieval has been successful, and I start out with 10 quality eggs (which is quite a few). I might choose to have the eggs frozen and transported. When they are thawed, two of the eggs have been damaged and are no longer viable. Then I would have 8 eggs. Next, the eggs are injected with sperm cells, but 3 eggs do not fertilize. Then I would have 5 embryos. Next, the doctor judges the quality of the embryos and determines that 3 of the embryos are not suitable for transfer to the surrogate. Then I would have 2 embryos. This would give me the opportunity for one transfer procedure using 2 embryos. If that attempt failed, I would be done unless I start over with a new egg retrieval, which would be a very costly setback. So you can see how important it can be to have a large number of eggs to start out. That said, if all goes well, it takes only one egg to produce a baby.

The creation of multiple embryos, many of which were unlikely to create a pregnancy, was a controversial matter. It struck me as significant when I learned that in traditional reproduction, it is completely natural and common for embryos to pass through and out of the uterine canal without attaching – thus destroying the embryo. It appeared that nature was choosy with the embryos it created, as well.

Designer Babies and Gender Selection

Max and Alex, you are boys. That's no better than being girls. Yet, unlike 99.99999% of people out there, your gender was not accidental. I've already mentioned the facts that before your birth, your generation of our family contained five girls with no boys, and that the family name was without a male heir. It's important for you to know that you were not changed into boys, but chosen. Your embryos developed exactly as they naturally were.

Probably since the dawn of humans, some parents-in-waiting have hoped for babies of a particular gender. Perhaps they had several children of one gender, and were hoping for one or more of the other. This was true in our family, a situation coined as "family balancing". Perhaps they sensed they would relate better to either a girl or a boy. Or, in some cases, perhaps their reasons were far less benign. Whatever their motivations, over the eons they came up with many methods of highly questionable effectiveness to increase the likelihood of a result that they preferred. Some of those methods included different positions during sex, also rituals, diets, dances, and prayer.

Much more recently, science determined that individual sperm cells were genetically either male (containing a "y" chromosome) or female (containing an "x" chromosome). Whichever sperm ended up fertilizing the egg determined the gender of the resulting baby. This makes it sound like choosing sperm was the sure-fire method such parents had been awaiting. The problem with this method is conducting a test to determine the gender of a sperm, destroys the sperm, rendering it useless for egg fertilization. A procedure called sperm sorting which used dye to help determine the gender of sperm cells was used quite a lot. But estimates for this technique's rate of accuracy were only 60 to 70% – nothing reliable.

According to my research, there was only one procedure that had come into use very recently, which practically guaranteed a chosen outcome. It is called PGD, or pre-implantation genetic diagnosis. In layman's terms, that meant the identification of genes in an embryo before it was transferred to a surrogate. With PGD, a single cell was removed from an embryo. That cell would be tested and, in the case of gender selection, determined to contain an x or y chromosome, with a 99% rate of accuracy. At that point, the gender of the embryo was essentially known. For parents preferring a child of a specific gender, only embryos of the preferred gender would be transferred to the surrogate mother. The age old dilemma of controlling the gender of one's baby had just been solved for the first time in human history. All of my other efforts in my quest to become a father had occurred simply to enable me to have what other traditional parents had – a baby. PGD offered me something more.

The most common use of PGD was screening for the presence of a host of genetic disorders or diseases such as Down's syndrome, trisomy 21, Huntington's disease, and cystic fibrosis *before* a pregnancy occurred. Alex and Max, unlike your naturally born peers, you were never at risk for any of these ailments.

The same technology could be used to identify and choose certain cosmetic characteristics in an embryo, such as eye, hair and skin color. One could not choose a characteristic that was not already genetically present in the embryo, which was something the embryo inherited from its mother or father. One could not yet change an embryo's genetic makeup. One could only identify traits and then select the embryo with the traits one preferred. At the time, using PGD for anything that was not tied to the health of the baby was quite controversial and banned in some countries for ethical reasons.

Mandy's Big Surprise!

In South Africa, my egg donor was being medically stimulated for the retrieval process still several weeks away. Again I was waiting, this time with excitement. My life at home and work went on with few people aware of the drama that was happening for me behind the scenes.

I was at lunch on a workday with one of my favorite colleagues who knew about my parenting project. Mandy was 39, a hard worker, and highly involved in charity work. Our personalities created an instant bond once we were introduced. Every now and then we would get out together for a bite.

On this occasion, amidst unnoteworthy conversation, Mandy mentioned she was pregnant. Pregnant! I think she wanted my honest reaction, untainted by high emotion in her announcement. I was shocked and enthusiastic, but tempered.

"Do you want this??" I asked.

Mandy was single. Her present position at the company was enough to provide for her. But her and a family? That seemed more questionable. She proceeded to explain to me the details of her recent relationship, which frankly sounded unimpressive. She was clearly unsure about what she was going to do. I explained to her how ironic it was that she had achieved by accident and for free something I was trying so hard to achieve for myself with huge amounts of effort and money. I think that must have made some impact.

A week later, we had lunch again. She told me all about how the pregnancy had propelled her relationship to a new level. She was not only pregnant. She was pregnant with twins! And, her partner wanted the babies. The two of them had decided to get serious, and build a quality home together for their children. I was happy for her and so relieved. The termination of her pregnancy would have seemed to me like a tragedy and such a horrible waste – going in the completely opposite direction from what I was valuing so greatly. In the weeks ahead, Mandy and I would share all the latest news as our stories developed.

A Frantic Journey

Alex and Max, I've already told you how incredibly unlikely it is, genetically, for you to be who you are. Aside from events in distant corners of the universe, many events occur right in our own lives that can forever change our futures. A story is told in my family of how one of my brothers, Martin, nearly died as a young child. He was 3 years old.

He, my eldest brother, and our father were standing on their unlit boat dock on the river one evening after dark at their home in Guyana. My dad had turned his attention away from the boys for a few seconds when he heard a small splash. When he turned around, Martin, who couldn't swim, had vanished without a trace. My dad quickly looked over the sides of the dock aided by his flashlight. Scanning the tea colored, piranha infested water, he just happened to make out what seemed to be blonde hair several inches below the surface. He instantly jumped in and pulled Martin out. No harm was done. Yet a difference of seconds could have changed all of our lives forever. Maybe the incident changed us all anyway. Indeed, probably everything that we do influences the future more than we could imagine. I bring up the story because it reminds me of the next part of my quest to fatherhood, which led me dramatically past such an event.

The IVF laboratory and my clinic were in Thailand. Yet, a number of procedures still had to take place over here, with me. I arranged health screenings, required by the Thai clinic, to be done by my doctor in Los Angeles. My doctor looked at me with confusion about what it was I was doing, even after I explained it. Ultimately she went along with the tests. I was screened for Hepatitis B and C, Syphilis, and HIV. My sperm was also tested for fertility. All tests came back with favorable results.

More weeks passed as the egg donor received her medication and was preparing for the egg retrieval. In fact, the time got away from me. I was waiting for a request from the Thai clinic for my frozen biological sample. It finally dawned on me that I should contact them. I was shocked to find that there was very little time left to do this. These people were the experts! They were supposed to tell me what to do and when.

You can't just make a biological deposit at home, stick it in the freezer, and send it via priority mail in a Styrofoam® cooler with a bunch of ice. The sample has to be cryogenically flash frozen, kept extremely cold using liquid nitrogen, and sent in a specialized liquid nitrogen cooled container. There are only a couple of shipping companies that do this. And it's expensive. For a moment, I pictured the frozen canister in a first class seat on a tourist plane, with extra legroom, and a cocktail with one of those little umbrella decorations. I checked the prices, and found that it would cost a bit more to send my frozen sperm than it would for me to travel to Thailand myself! However, when I factored in the time, trouble, and expenses I would incur making the trip personally, sending frozen specimen still made sense.

After a few calls, I located a local fertility clinic that would help me with this task. I quickly made arrangements to deposit my biological sample (sperm). I entered the clinic, wondering if these nice folks would have been helping me had they known I was gay. I certainly didn't volunteer that information on the phone after all the trouble I had in my dealings with local clinics earlier. I will spare you most of the details of this proceeding. It occurred much the way one would expect. It involved a little room and a small plastic container. I will say that the young lady that showed me to my room seemed unnecessarily cold. I don't think she suspected that I was gay. I'm a little hard to pick out. I did wonder if she had been the recipient of unwelcome comments, winks or the like from men who were being shown to a room to make such a deposit.

The room was so small one could barely turn around. It contained an oddly-large, leathery chair and a small stack of "special" magazines, all aimed towards straight men, of course. There was a fancy, flat-screen TV with especially appropriate visual material pre-loaded – so I was told. I couldn't make the thing work, which is ironic given that I'm supposed to be good with that kind of stuff. Anyway, I was just being curious.

I had been told that I was expected to complete my responsibilities in the room without delay. So I prepared the sample and handed it through a window, directly to a woman in the cryogenics lab. She was dressed like a doctor going into surgery, face covering and all. Puffs of white liquid nitrogen vapor surrounded her. It was really quite impressive.

If this worked, a tiny bit of the contents of that cup would be handed back to me in a little over 9 months in the form of a baby. What a miracle that would be! When I left the building, it felt a little bit like I had dropped someone off at the airport!

The frozen sperm was picked up hours later by a specialized carrier, DHL. There were only a handful of days left to get the shipment to the clinic in Thailand. I was aware the liquid nitrogen could only keep the sample properly frozen for about 5 days. So I was alarmed when, on day 3, I received word that the package was halted in customs as it was entering the country. The authorities needed some kind of license documentation from my Thai clinic before they would let the container pass. For two days I worriedly made calls to the Thai clinic and shipping company to try to smooth things out. Again and again I received word that the shipment had not arrived and the document had not been received.

How long would the liquid nitrogen stay cold? Could the contents of the canister arrive partially thawed and of questionable quality? These questions plagued my mind as I waited, basically helpless. This was not a box of doughnuts! This was potentially my future child! In my mind, I pictured an inconspicuous five-gallon, plastic, liquid nitrogen cooler collecting dust in a hot, muggy room at the Bangkok cargo terminal. The last few drops of condensation formed a wet spot on the carpet below, as it was buried and forgotten under other wayward shipments. A failure for one more day, and I would be forced to get on a plane to Thailand to personally make the biological deposit.

I had never been out of the country on my own. I had no idea how feasible such a last minute and enormously-long trip would be. If *that* strategy failed, there would be no sperm available for the freshly gathered eggs, the retrieval of which could not be delayed. My best shot of becoming a father could be needlessly gone forever.

Finally, with the clock running short, I received a short email stating that Thai customs had received the paperwork they were requesting from the clinic and the shipment went through. The precious cargo had been saved! I could finally breathe a sigh of relief.

Action

Things began to happen very fast! Before this time, it could be weeks between emails with Thailand. Suddenly, I was being updated sometimes more than once per day. This was exciting, yet stressful. Each piece of correspondence had the potential of getting me a step closer to fatherhood or informing me that a particular hurdle could not be overcome, and my quest was at its end.

My egg donor, Roxanne, flew in from South Africa (where she was living) and made the egg donation. I was elated to receive the news that 20 eggs had been retrieved. That was a lot!

Within a day or two, the eggs were injected with sperm (ICSI). I was extremely excited to hear that all 20 eggs had fertilized. A day or two later, I was less impressed that out of 20 fertilizations, the doctor concluded that only eight resulting embryos were considered normal. The PGD (pre-implantation genetic diagnosis) was done. Of the eight embryos, six were male, two were female. I had requested that the sperm be sorted for maleness before the PGD, which apparently explained why there were more male embryos than female. So with 20 eggs originally received, after all of the steps had been taken, I had a total of eight embryos that qualified for transfer to the womb of the surrogate immediately. If each transfer utilized two embryos, I would have the opportunity for four transfer attempts, which I considered deeply fortunate.

You might think I forgot to choose a surrogate mother – the person who would carry you to term. Remember, this person was generally different from the egg donor. In this case, the surrogate was provided and chosen by the clinic.

Some intended parents have a particular person in mind to carry the baby – maybe a relative or close friend. In my case, I actually had a sister-in-law who was generously ready, willing, and very capable. There were a few important qualities to consider when choosing a surrogate. To maximize the odds of reaching the finish line with a healthy baby and surrogate, she would preferably be in her twenties to early thirties with a history of at least one healthy, prior pregnancy. She would exhibit good all-round health, doctor examined of course, with no smoking and the ability to abstain entirely from alcohol during the pregnancy. She would be carrying the child for many months, so it was important that she be a responsible person with a healthy diet and lifestyle.

It was in the clinic's interests to achieve a healthy birth for its clients, and their database of surrogates were pre-screened for all of the attributes mentioned above. So I was very comfortable letting the clinic make this choice.

I gave the go ahead for the first transfer of two male embryos to the womb of my surrogate, Ponsai (pronounced, Pon-si). A photograph of these two embryos, under the microscope, was sent to me. I gazed at that photograph for some time, amazed. Was this the first glimpse I would ever have of a future child, or children? Not many parents get to see their children *before* the pregnancy.

A handful of days later I received an email with the subject line, "Positive pregnancy test". I gasped when I saw it. I clutched my computer tablet, nearly tearing up. It was minutes before I opened and read the email. I wanted to live in that moment for a time before moving on, afraid that the email would say something different than I understood from the subject line. Yet, it was true. The first chemical test for pregnancy had been completed and was definitively positive.

I thought to myself, "After all of the bumps along the way, I achieved a pregnancy on my first try!"

I was speaking with my brother, Martin, on the phone around that time. He and his wife had been through one round of IVF years earlier with no luck. I had not been announcing on a loud speaker the results of the first test, because I still considered it unverified. So he had not yet heard. When I finally and calmly got around to telling him that one test had been done and had come back positive, he was shocked.

"Really?!" Martin remarked with amazement.

This was feeling more real to me all the time. A week or so later, a second chemical test was done, which was also positive.

Three weeks after the transfer, on July 4, 2013, I received the first ultrasound via email. It was the first time I read the words "fetus A" and "fetus B." Two fetuses! I am still moved to tears today when I think about that moment. Again, I gazed and wondered about my future children.

The next day, I called my parents from work and told them, "I have news. The ultrasound has happened. The pregnancy is normal. And there are (pausing for effect) two fetuses."

I could hear my mom and dad on the other end cheering and laughing.

"Twins!" My brother George, who was visiting them, heard the commotion and inquired. "What?" he hollered. That phone call was one of the proudest and most joyful moments of my life.

There I was, not so far along with the pregnancy. It was exciting, yet also nerve wracking. I felt pulled in two directions. One side wanted to celebrate. The other told me to wait. I continued my late night walks, pondering the future, feeling like I was walking a tightrope. On one side was a future as a father of twins, on the other an abyss of the unknown, perhaps just the solitary life I had been living.

I expressed the discomfort of not knowing in an email update to my Aunt Carole, my mom's sister. She wrote me back something that resonated. She said to love the process.

"Love the process, and you won't need to be so concerned about results." My aunt had always been known for being a bit on the ultra-creative side. Yet I was grasping for anything to soothe my mind. This helped.

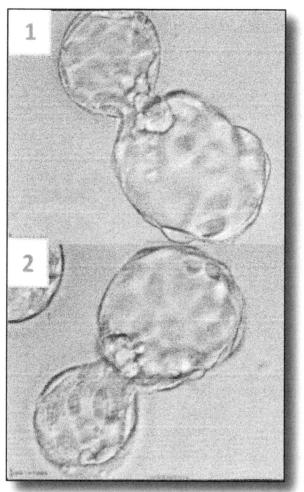

This is a magnified image of the actual 2 embryos that were used in the first transfer to the surrogate mother.

Tragedy

As the days passed, I tried to avoid worrying about the pregnancy. It wasn't easy. While talking with people I knew, though it was constantly on my mind, I tried to avoid even using the term *miscarriage*. I didn't want to do anything that might disrupt the pregnancy, even though I didn't consider myself to be a superstitious person.

A text message came in from Mandy, my co-worker. She had been pregnant with her twins now for almost three months. We had continued our comparing-notes lunches together. We loved to dream about how our two sets of twins would play together – being practically the same age. I was completely unprepared for what I saw on my phone.

"I lost the babies," the text message read. My heart sank. We had talked a number of times about this possibility. We knew it was not uncommon. We were both hoping that the warnings were exaggerated as a comfort to grieving mothers, and that nine months would fly on by without mishap.

Mandy wasn't in the mood to talk much about it. Eventually we got together for another lunch. Apparently, even after less than three months, mothers who experience miscarriage are given the opportunity to see their babies. Mandy described the perfectly shaped miniature parts and saying goodbye to the two children who were not to be. It is hard for me to imagine the emotional gravity of such an encounter.

Suddenly, I was thrown very unapologetically into the reality of my worst fears regarding my pregnancy. A positive pregnancy test was *not* a guaranteed birth. A healthy ultrasound was *not* a guaranteed birth. Even a four or five month healthy pregnancy report would be no guarantee that I would live out my days as a father. Like Mandy, my surrogate was carrying twins, an inherently more risky pregnancy scenario.

I told others parents about my fears and they gave me the harsh truth, a parent *never* really stops worrying. A parent never knows what tomorrow will bring. No matter how healthy or old a child may be, they or anyone could meet an untimely death at any time. It was just a part of life.

Traditional parents usually had the chance to easily try again if a pregnancy didn't work out. For those of us dependent on the lab with limited budgets, opportunities were few. Each attempt could be our last.

I continued to pray for the health of my fetuses and my surrogate. In my mind, I was on a train with no brakes, bound for home, on an unfamiliar and possibly unreliable track. The rails ahead extended into the fog and out of sight.

A Gift for My Surrogate

Ponsai, my surrogate, was just one month into the pregnancy. I wanted so much to skip the next four or five months to a date when we could have more confidence. For me the days drew out like a sword from its sheath.

I did not have a rapport with Ponsai, for various reasons, including the fact that she spoke no English. I felt a strong urge to communicate how deeply important her services were to me, and to express my appreciation for her, personally. I resolved to send her a heartfelt letter, and enough money for her to purchase something she would really like, as a token gift. My case worker at the clinic made the arrangements. After looking, Ponsai chose a gold ring that she was particularly fond of. She shared that the ring was something she could always wear to remind her of her surrogacy. The letter I sent is below:

"Dear Ponsai,

My name is Joseph. I am the intended parent for the babies you are carrying.

It is a great honor to be able to send you this message. I do not know very much about you, but I do know that you have given generously of yourself to help me make my dream of parenthood a reality – something I have wanted for many years. I am so very thankful for the gift of your service!

Please accept this gold ring (of your choosing) as a token of my appreciation. We will likely not correspond much during the pregnancy. But please know that you will be in my thoughts each day over the coming weeks and months.

With my most sincere appreciation,

Joseph (and family)"

I realized the letter and gift for Ponsai was no guarantee that the pregnancy would go smoothly. Yet, my case worker told me that she had been ecstatic to receive it. I felt more confident knowing that my surrogate had a sense of how precious she was to me.

Moving in Mom and Dad

It was September. We were three months into the pregnancy and, although it was no sure thing yet, so far all was going well. I felt it was time for me to start making some tangible changes around the house in preparation for twin babies.

Being single, through the early years of planning, I had expected to hire a live-in nanny who would care for the babies when I was at work. Early in the year, late in my search for the egg donor, my parents actually started voicing their desire to help personally. They didn't just want to visit often and babysit. They wanted to sell their beautiful house in North Carolina, move in with me, and make their new grandchild (now grandsons) the center of the next chapter in their lives. They were both retired *and* still healthy enough for this kind of responsibility to be realistic. Although impressed by their enthusiasm and generosity, I was not convinced that their moving into my house with me was a good idea. My mother and I are both somewhat controlling and territorial people when it comes to the home. I saw conflict as inevitable. However, it was not long before I could not ignore the immense advantages included with my parents in the home with me, helping with the kids. So I signed off on the deal.

My parents' house did not sell immediately, which made for some stress. Ultimately, a qualified buyer did come forward, and the deal was done. The last of my spare room renters moved out. My parents sold off most of their stuff, journeyed all the way across the country and moved into "Stagg Manor," my home, affectionately and lightheartedly named by the street it is on.

Alex and Max, some day you may understand how a person can love someone deeply and simultaneously be very adversarial with them. I pray this doesn't describe your relationship with me over time. I love your grandmother so much that it sometimes makes me cry just thinking about it. Yet she and I are very stubborn about how we like things to be around our home. For the first time since I left for college, she and I were again living under the same roof. But this time, I was in charge. Something she clearly hadn't come to terms with.

The first couple of weeks with Mom were *not comfortable*. This was a big worry! My mom wasn't in the house ten hours before making demands about changing key features of *my home*! She wanted to completely reorganize the décor around the fireplace and replace wall hangings. And this was not a suggestion. This was an outright demand!

Now I could understand if my home was filled with inappropriate, dorm-room-quality vulgarity that would be inappropriate for children. This was nice stuff, which I had arranged with a great deal of thought, consideration, and I cared very much about! After years of living under my parents' thumbs at home (appropriately), I took a great deal of pride in this place being mine.

My mother had the gall at one point, when I started locking the door to my private bedroom, to demand unfettered access 24 hours a day! That was never going to happen. We argued feverishly about it twice, with my dad sensibly taking my side. To this day, I continue to lock my door whenever I want, sometimes just to exercise the right.

I guess dealing with all of this was the price I had to pay to have my parents so thoroughly involved in my endeavor. It was obvious they were making my audacious dream of parenthood truly feasible. As much as I wanted to assert my authority in my house, I would have to be flexible. I still stood my ground on many topics, but relinquished some. I knew organization in the kitchen was not going to stick with me, so I gave up that room immediately and almost entirely.

The conflicts came frequently over the first month, but gradually subsided. Two months in, we were in a state of virtual harmony, or at least a long held cease fire. Though I was occasionally not impressed with the day-to-day menu, it had been a long time since I had had such consistent, home-cooked food. That was a wonderful perk.

I was also extremely pleased to have my parents so near at this very special time in my life, as they were getting older. My dad was already pushing 80 with Mom just four years behind.

From left to right: Dennis, Jeanie and Joseph Hahle.

Preparing for Newborns

It was late November. The pregnancy, now in its fifth month, continued to go smoothly. The weeks kept passing by. Planning for an epic trip to Thailand was well underway.

My dad and I were putting a lot of work into an aggressive remodeling of the main bathroom on the first floor of the house. We were determined to do the remodel entirely ourselves, to save money, despite never having done most of that kind of work before. The bathroom had always been sub-par. With my parents moving in and babies on the way, that room was really going to be used. A lot! We also figured that once the babies arrived, we would be so busy with baby care, and dependent on the room, it would be years before the remodeling could be done. So Dad and I went right to work demolishing most of what was there with a hammer and crowbar. All of the fixtures were being replaced and moved to different positions in the room. So the tile, the drywall, even the subfloor was going away. We had all new plumbing and electrical work ahead of us. When you opened the door, all you saw was two-by-four studs, floor joists, and the bare ground.

Obviously, the bathroom was entirely shut down. Depending on how things turned out, it would be weeks or even months of hard work before it could be used again. We were rolling the dice a bit. Technically this was an experiment. An early homecoming for the babies might be a complete mess if we could not get the room back together in a timely manner.

I came home from work one night quite displeased. The leadership of the TV show that I had been editing sent me home early one episode with no word on my next project. Basically, I was losing five weeks of scheduled work with no new start date set. Unexpected gaps in employment were not uncommon in my profession. I knew I would be facing a period of time when I could not work as soon as the babies were born, which I had prepared for. Yet, this was just November! Now I was dealing with the likelihood of a much longer break from my income than expected. I would simply have to have faith and move forward.

On Thanksgiving Day, my brother Martin and his family, and my Uncle John and his family were with us. At the main meal, my dad gave the blessing. He included the twins, "…at this exciting time, as we anticipate two babies in formation in Thailand…" Shivers ran up my spine. Practically every adult in the family had children. This was the first time that *my* children were being acknowledged during a family gathering.

December rolled in. We had a baby shower planned for the end of the month. I went with my mom to the local Babies"R"Us® to buy some things, most importantly a stroller. There were a gob to choose from, and these things, especially the double ones, were pretty complicated. They supposedly attached seamlessly with various car seats. I wanted to know what I was about to spend $300 on. So I went to work attempting to test all of the strollers; folding them down and attaching seats in various configurations. At least that was the idea. Nothing seemed to work! I was interested in a big, double stroller that would cover all of those needs until the boys were five or so years old. Mom was also there to *help*, trying to push me towards the smaller, more lightweight, individual strollers. I had parts and seats and hoods and all kinds of junk strewn about the isle, trying to figure out what attached to what, and what to buy. After at least an hour of intense frustration, getting seemingly nowhere, I stuck the stuff back on the shelf. I announced we were retreating before I had some kind of melt down. A day or two later, I found a stroller online from the same store that looked good, and just went with it.

There were so many little things that we needed, and so many choices at the stores. It was really quite overwhelming. I felt that when we needed something we didn't think of, we could always just run out and get it. We were still looking for two cribs. Otherwise, the nursery was basically ready, having received a new coat of paint and drapes from my mom, and a new, double-sized bed for someone to keep a close eye on the babies on certain nights.

I visited the local Thai embassy with my parents to apply for tourist visas. This was legally required for anyone visiting Thailand from the U.S. While there, we had the opportunity to ask some questions about various things. We had been hearing in the news about a few isolated incidents in Thailand where opponents of the Thai government had recently been injured or killed during a demonstration. We wondered whether or not this was something we should be concerned about. Occasional incidents of violence for political reasons are, after all, not uncommon in the world. The officials we talked to said it was not a problem, and asked when we were planning to make our trip. When we said we were going in late January, they both chuckled lightly and said the disruptions would be long forgotten by then. We each wondered if that was really true, and kept our eyes on the incoming headlines.

The hugely time-consuming bathroom remodel seemed to be coming along extremely well, thanks in large part to the extra time I had due to my unexpected break from editing. This project was turning out to be a great way for my dad and me to practice being a team. I was doing most of the new copper plumbing while he did the drainpipes. He connected most of the new fixtures while I handled the electrical work. We took turns with the tile. One of us would make the cuts while the other mortared the tiles in place. With a bit of luck, the new bathroom would be open for business by Christmas, just about a week away.

A pregnancy report came in about half way through December, on par with those we had received every few weeks since the start. The babies were estimated at almost 3 pounds each. You had two and a half months to go to be full term. I felt we were entering a period in which you could potentially survive the birth if it happened early. My research had actually shown that babies born at just five months, and only one pound or even less, had survived birth. Still, I was looking for something more dependable and healthy. It was an uncomfortable place to be – anticipating, but not really knowing.

We remained most hopeful and prayerfully optimistic.

Baby Names

For a couple of years I had been thinking a lot about baby
names. It wasn't the most important thing, but it *was* something
that would be stamped on your forehead presumably for the rest
of your lives. So I figured it was worth some thought.

I would brainstorm lists of names and think about whether
or not I liked them. I found that I really liked very, very few. My
child would be special. So his or her name would need to stand
out. For me, that ruled out simple, popular American names like
Mark or Adam. A few more uncommon names like Rafael
appealed to me. Friends I bounced that off of were quick to
express that a name like Rafael points to a very specific ethnicity.
If my child did not bear that ethnicity, it would be strange for
him to bear that name. You also want a name that will not be
easy for other kids to make fun of. I enjoyed joking with my
friends that I was considering a ridiculous name like Quimby,
Aladdin, or Neo. Neo almost made it as a middle name. One also
wants to choose a name that rolls together nicely with the last
name. So Rafael Hahle (Hāle) wasn't destined then for two
reasons. There were plenty of names I came across that sounded
good in full length, but were less attractive to me in their
abbreviation. I liked Daniel, but not so much just Dan. I liked
William, but not so much just Bill.

James was the front running name for almost two years
straight. In the end, after a bit of waffling, the names Alexander
and Maximus won out. The full-length names were strong and

ornate. And their various abbreviations, "Alex, Max, Xander, and Maxim" all appealed to me. For the most part, I just really liked the sounds.

The middle names proved to be even more fun, as this name was more easily hidden, and so more available for creativity. When I was about nine years old, I saw an incredible children's movie, *The Never Ending Story*, which stirred up in me a sense of adventure unlike I had ever known before. The main character was a young Indian brave named Atreyu. He was on an epic quest in a world of the imagination. His story is told in a book that the other main character, a boy in the real world named Bastian, is reading. These two characters made a lasting impact on me. Their names just happen to be super cool, as well. So the names were chosen: Alexander Atreyu would be the first born and Maximus Bastian, the second.

I showed this movie to my parents before our trip. I think they enjoyed it, particularly my mom. The film had a strange effect on me. I actually found myself choked up and teary, almost from beginning to end. It was quite bizarre.

That Amazing, Terrifying Day

One morning, a few days after Christmas, the alarm went off. I pulled myself out of bed. Actually, first I hit the snooze button at least twice. Then I slowly wrestled myself up and out. It was December 28, 2013. The baby shower party was the very next day, so I had a few things to prepare for that. I had finished the last major work on the bathroom remodel just the day before. So that was no longer an issue. I was still in my bathrobe when I sat down on the sofa in my room and grabbed my computer tablet to get a stock market update and check my email.

There it was: the email that would change my life.

I froze. My stunned eyes were glued to the words of the message in front of me. "Surrogate mother Ponsai was admitted into the hospital at 3:00 am for contractions and doctor had to do C section immediately."

I swallowed and continued to stare. I was a dad. Yet, this was not supposed to happen for two more months! All of the planning, all of the expense, all of the worry, all of the dreams… It was possibly all unraveling six thousand miles away, and there was absolutely nothing I could do about it.

You were out in the world early. Would you survive? I scanned the email again and again, hoping there had been some misunderstanding. Maybe the email had been sent to the wrong parent? Maybe my worry had inspired an uncomfortable dream? It would certainly not have been the first nightmare. No. There was no mistake. Baby "A" was just over four pounds and baby

"B" was just under four pounds. As small as you were, these weights were quite good for infants born at just 31 weeks, or about two months early. Precious little more was revealed about your condition.

I stood up and crept down the stairs in my bathrobe with that same dazed look on my face and a knot forming in my throat. I entered the doorway of my father's study where he was going about some business on his computer.

"Dad, I have news." I said quietly and deliberately. "The babies have been born." He turned to me, reacting with surprise and a bit more enthusiasm than I could muster from myself. He had plenty of questions, but I had few answers. The email was extremely brief.

The whole world had changed in a moment. Everything I was going to be doing that day was instantly put on hold. The usual morning rituals proceeded – now interwoven with discussions about how we would deal with the new situation. Many emotions were bombarding me as I sat at my desk to make a journal entry.

"I'm amazed at the thought of being a father, and quite concerned about the babies' health. We are honestly a bit shocked at how early Alex and Max have come. And we are trying to adjust our planning for a much earlier trip to Thailand than expected. As I write this, I am holding back tears. I know that these babies are now out on their own. They no longer have the warmth and security of their mother's womb. It may be uncomfortable for them. And they may even have a sense of being alone. And that makes me uncomfortable. I want to be there with them. I want them to know how much I love them, and how well they are going to be cared for."

At some point before noon I wandered into the backyard and happened across an old, bird's nest that had fallen to the ground. Lying there was a tiny, little, blue egg with brown speckles. It was hollow. In the five and a half years living in my house, I had never found an egg in my yard before that day. I couldn't help feeling the egg was some sort of acknowledgement of my experience. This egg had fallen from the tree, a departure from its plan, just as you had been born early. Somehow, this was a comfort to me.

This is the actual egg that was found that day.

Max and Alex, I'd always pictured the day of my child's birth in a classic way: a speedy trip to the hospital, cries from mother and baby, handing out chocolate cigars, and peering at you fondly through a big window as you squirmed and cooed. As with many things in life, the reality made itself known in a big and unpredictable way.

Every time we celebrate your birthday, I will think back to this day and how uncomfortable it was. I wasn't with you. I couldn't see you. I didn't even know if you would survive. This memory is just one of many that will regularly remind me of how precious your lives are, and how special the time is that I have to share with you, face to face.

We awaited more reassuring news from Thailand as we prepared to leave within the next few days.

The Baby Shower

All our thoughts were on Thailand. Yet, the baby shower was supposed to be the next day. I was dreading this. A baby shower was supposed to be fun and happy. How could I feel that with you boys born way early and possibly fighting for your lives? These were not circumstances appropriate for a frivolous celebration in my mind, but preparations had been made and guests were coming. We had just enough time to squeeze this in before our trip. So, the show was going on.

To my surprise, as soon as people started to show up, I started giving house tours and was feeling pretty good. Many more folks came than I expected. Several of my personal friends were there. Also a number of my former, spare-room tenants were present. There were a few of my work friends, and a large-handful of people from our church. All of them stayed a long time.

Mom had baked and prepared some terrific food. Dad read a psalm from the Bible and said a prayer. I then made a short speech, becoming quite emotional and blubbery towards the end, as I told the crowd how lucky you both were to have such a wonderful extended family. Justified or not, I'm quite embarrassed about that now. As even-tempered as I am known to be, in recent years, I sure can find myself sobbing if I'm touched emotionally in the right way. That's just not something people in our family are known to do.

By the time the crowds had left, we were buried in gifts and cards, which we opened immediately. The party had distracted my mind for a good few hours and left me feeling very warm – something I really needed.

Now that the music was turned off, it was back to reality. We had a miraculous crisis on our hands. From that point forward, every moment was focused on getting to you.

Our Trip to the Moon

Monday was a whirlwind of packing and arranging. I think we managed to clean up a little after the baby shower. The Christmas decorations, including the tree, would have to wait. Honestly, my memory of this period is a bit foggy. I do know I was frustrated and anxious. Standard activities like meals had to go on. Yet it just didn't feel right. Every moment we weren't with you felt like neglect.

On Tuesday morning we were off to the airport. My neighbor friend, Tom, was good enough to drive us. All was well until we were told we had been dropped off at the wrong terminal, Air China. This was not Tom's fault. Thankfully, he quickly got us to China Airlines, where we were supposed to be.

The journey was to take us through Taipei, Taiwan, and was expected to encompass about 21 hours. It unfolded like a gauntlet, each step forward including a little challenge to be overcome. We were following the sun. As soon as it slowly slipped over the western horizon, the darkness following seemed to last forever.

I was more and more miserable as the hours passed due to confinement, sleep deprivation, and waves of anxiety about your health. Believe it or not, shortly after the birth, the Thai clinic closed down for the holidays. So, I could hardly get any updates! One message that did get through stated "baby B" had a heart defect. There was almost no explanation. I couldn't make the plane go any faster, so there was nothing I could do but wait!

Our departing gate in Taipei was in a large room, which was practically deserted. There must have been a problem with the plumbing somewhere nearby because the room smelled like an open sewer.

An entry officer at the Bangkok airport, who spoke little English, gave us some trouble in a vacant and dimly lit corridor. I'm not sure if he was armed, but it sure felt like it. We had brought our new baby car seats from Los Angeles in their original boxes. The officer asked us if they were new. We replied, "Yes." The car seats had been purchased *recently*. Somehow, he assumed they had been purchased during the trip, and demanded their value be taxed. I was trying with futility to explain the misunderstanding to him when my dad plucked down the 60 dollar duty he was demanding. Then we coasted on through.

Dad explained shortly after, that when on such trips, it was wise to just do what they say in such matters. He was right. We certainly didn't need to create an international incident over $60 and a couple of infant car seats. This was a tiny bump on the way to much more important things.

We made it outside to a large area where many people were standing in line to get cab rides. We had too much bulky stuff to ever fit into one of those vehicles, even the mini vans. So we had to jettison something. The car seats were removed from their bulky cardboard boxes, which we quietly folded down and, with no other good options in sight, stuffed under a nearby bench.

After more confusion and waiting through a very long line, we secured a private van to take us into the city. It was still night. The freeways and streets were deserted. I tell you, it felt like the dark side of the moon, chugging along in that old minivan on the *wrong* side of the road, so far from home, with a complete stranger who spoke no English, bearing only as much as we could carry, and moving farther and farther into the unknown. One easily got the feeling that if something went wrong, no one could help us, and there would be no way to escape. We might just vanish halfway around the world without anyone we knew ever knowing what happened to us.

Thankfully, our driver was true. We arrived at our apartment in central, metropolitan Bangkok, which we were thankful was open at 1:30 in the morning. The clerk took us to our room on the third floor. The unit was stale, with a bit of an odd, smoky smell and a few things here and there not really working. There was beautiful, light-stained wood paneling. There were two bedrooms, one bath, and one small living/dining area. The closest thing to a kitchen was a microwave and refrigerator just outside the bathroom. We had chosen the apartment largely for its impressive economy and close proximity to the hospital. So its modesty was not a huge surprise.

In my fatigue, I decided I needed a shower. I got undressed and entered the bathroom. After closing the door, a bright, green shape about seven inches long shot off the wall, darted across the room and then disappeared out of sight. I saw it just long enough to realize that it was some kind of lizard or gecko. It quickly became apparent there was no sense searching for it. It was long gone.

I spent several minutes standing in the tub, trying to figure out how it worked. There were some extra knobs and pipes. The most striking difference from what we had at home was an electric, water-heating box right above the showerhead that the water passed through before spraying out. I came to learn somewhat later that these units were common in that part of the world. I didn't realize at first that there was a limit to how fast the box could heat the water, and if the water were flowing quickly, it wouldn't get very hot at all. So my first shower in Bangkok was unfortunately tepid.

The sunrise was coming soon. So in a zombie-like state, we crashed.

The Day I Met My Children

I woke to that somewhat odd stale scent I had noticed the night before in our apartment. Light was bursting through the window. I could hear the faint sounds of heavy city traffic. After a quick bite to eat and getting ourselves together, we stepped out of the apartment on our first expedition. Of course, I wanted to see the two of you and fast. Unfortunately, a couple things had to pre-empt. First, we needed to visit the clinic to meet with Na, who was in charge of my individual case. The clinic was located across the street on the 21st floor of a modern and impressive office building. So we started in that direction on foot.

Bangkok was no longer the dark side of the moon. Ten million residents strong, this place was bustling and colorful. Narrow, old, side streets and alleys, often lined with a patchwork of busy street vendors, flowed into wide, six-lane, main streets that were crammed with noisy cars and motorcycles. There were lots of colorful taxis, some of them bright pink. A look up revealed a forest of towering modern skyscrapers. I remember the smell being particularly strong, probably a mixture of unfamiliar foods and deep fat being prepared by the street vendors, along with apparently stagnant, decrepit water in the many canals honeycombed through the city. It was also very humid.

We reached the clinic office, which had freshly reopened after their holiday break, and were asked to wait for my coordinator. They offered us coffee, which we welcomed. Three very small, neatly-presented cups arrived with a little bit of liquid at the bottom. The coffee was extremely strong. Though that made the coffee almost unbearable, something about it was delightful at the same time. I came to find that this was the standard for coffee in Bangkok. In fact, we never came across the kind of coffee or tea that we were familiar with at home.

As we sat in the waiting room, I noticed a Thai girl, who reminded me greatly of a picture I had seen of my surrogate, sitting across from us. Later, the meeting began, and she was brought in and introduced to us. It was Ponsai, your surrogate mother. Alex and Max, I'm sure you cannot help but be curious about this woman. She was your birth mother. For seven straight months she carried you in her womb. We know extremely little about her life, day to day. Yet, we do know that during that time, as she ate a meal, socialized with friends, slept in her bed, went to the grocery store, walked here and there in Bangkok; you were right there inside her. We also know that she had a family of her own, with at least one child. While our face-to-face time with her was very brief, I am happy to share my impressions. She was quiet and very sweet looking, with mannerisms that struck me as modest and proper. Her build was petite. Her dark hair was medium long and quite straight. I could imagine she would have made a treasured friend, had the opportunity been present and practical. We all took a turn hugging her and expressing our deep appreciation for what she had done for us. Our conversation had to be translated by Na, as Ponsai did not speak any English. She seemed to be moving about amazingly well considering five days earlier she had just been through a C-section birth of twins.

We discussed relevant business and were given advice about how to live and care for the babies in Bangkok. Honestly though, I had a hard time paying close attention because I couldn't take my mind off of you.

At long last, it was time to see you in person, my beloved babies, for the first time. The hospital was located just four blocks away. So the five of us proceeded, again on foot. It was very hard to hold myself back from running. As well as she was doing, Ponsai was still quite sore and walking slowly. I kept finding myself stuck in the middle of the group, lagging behind Na and my father who were pulling way ahead to wait for Ponsai and my mom, who were trailing far behind.

We reached the hospital and headed straight to the seventh floor. I was fitted with a simple, white, hospital gown and led, without the others, into the NICU (Neonatal Intensive Care Unit). I had received reports and descriptions of your condition. How your appearance would really strike me was yet a mystery. After well over a year of working entirely remotely to become a father, this was the first time I would ever see you, my children.

I passed through the first room which was full of babies on carts, perhaps fifteen or twenty, many of them crying. The nurses appeared to be exclusively Thai women, many of them quite young. The next room was full of babies too. Some of these were receiving examinations, being changed, or maybe just arriving. Clear at the back of the department, I was taken through a door into a room that was much quieter and less brightly lit. There was a lot of complicated-looking technology. Following the nurse, I approached two, clear plastic enclosures (incubators), which were each roughly the size and shape of a medium-size dog travel carrier. I dared to peek inside, and saw two very small, but not tiny, pink babies, clad in very loose fitting white gowns.

Alex, you were labeled "Baby A." You were on your side, facing somewhat down. You had a tiny feeding tube going into your mouth and, I was told, an IV at your naval.

Max, the label on your incubator read "Baby B." The top section of your incubator had been replaced with a plastic wrap sort of material, and more of your surroundings had been improvised to meet your unique needs. You were more on your stomach with your head turned slightly to the side. You didn't look particularly comfortable. With a feeding tube *and* ventilator tube at your mouth, it was more difficult to see your face.

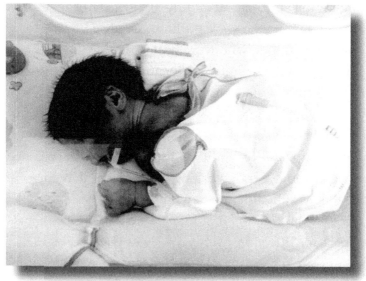

"Baby A", Alexander Hahle. January 2nd, 2014.

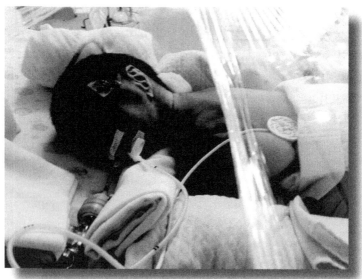

"Baby B", Maximus Hahle. January 2nd, 2014.

Both of you had a lot of dark brown hair and a surprising amount of fur on your upper backs and arms – something that seemed odd to me at the time. I later discovered that this hair, called lanugo, was temporary and actually common in babies born prematurely.

At the nurse's instruction, I rubbed sterilizing fluid on my hands, reached through a little door in the enclosures and touched each of you, very gently. Alex, I touched your back. Max, I touched your head. You were so soft, it was hard to even tell you were there. I was very careful not to disturb you. After going through so much, I didn't want to do anything that could make your delicate lives more difficult. Each breath appeared to be a challenge.

The feeling I had was unlike anything I had ever experienced or expected. I saw and felt myself in you two boys. In a surreal way, I felt like you *were* me, like I was in three places in the room at one time. Part of this must have come from knowing you existed because of my actions, and you were entirely my responsibility, yet the feeling was more like what could be described as time-travel. It was as if I had traveled back in time to witness my own birth.

Mom and Dad came in next. Then later, Ponsai came and looked. Everyone seemed quite pleased.

We spoke with the doctor, who appeared very competent. While she was fairly upbeat, she described an upward climb the two of you would face over the coming weeks as you hopefully gained strength. She noted the condition of each of you, remarking with special urgency about the heart impairment in Max that I had been emailed about earlier. The impairment, PDA or patent ductus arteriosus, is a congenital heart defect. Put very simply, this is a natural artery in the fetus that diverts blood away from the lungs, sending it directly to the body. It usually closes on its own shortly after birth. Sometimes, with premature babies it doesn't close, and dangerously limits proper function of the lungs. PDA was the reason Max required a breathing tube. Max's heart specialist said he would start him on a special medication. If the medication failed, surgery might be required.

The thought of surgery for you, Max, was extremely hard to swallow. This tiny baby, my son, had been ejected from his mother's womb two months early. That wasn't your fault! Once you were out, you were struggling with each breathe just to stay alive, with two plastic tubes going into your mouth and taped over your face. And now, they might have to surgically open your chest? How could you survive such a thing? It seemed merciless. I tried not to think about the surgery and focused on the thought of the medicine doing its work.

We were instructed to visit the cashier on the way out. As far as I could tell, it was not possible to purchase insurance in Thailand to cover this type of medical need. In my circumstances, my personal health coverage from the U.S. wouldn't pay for birth related medical care for infants overseas. So I knew any charges from the hospital were going to come straight out of my pocket. The cashier handed me the receipt. The number at the bottom read ฿316,000. This certainly didn't sound good. The receipt had been issued in Thai Baht, which I knew had a dramatically lower value than a U.S. dollar. After converting the figure, just over $10,000, which I put on my credit card, paid for the birth procedure, including C-section, care for the surrogate mother, and the first five days of intensive care for both of you. This was manageable.

The scary part was projecting the cost of intensive care for you into the future. The doctor's rough estimate for how long you would both need to be at the hospital was eight weeks. Of course, I would do whatever was necessary. Yet, if that scenario played out, the cost would be backbreaking! I continued to focus on how fortunate we were, five days after the birth, to have two babies alive. I hoped and prayed for the best.

The U.S. Consulate

That same, first day in Bangkok, my parents and I said goodbye to Na and Ponsai before exiting the hospital. We needed to begin our dealings with the U.S. Consulate. Before the trip, I had studied on a map the location of the consulate and various places that would be of interest to us. None of our phones worked in that country, so we were dependent on old-fashioned techniques for navigation. I remembered the Consulate being fairly close, so we proceeded again on foot. Thirty minutes, and two or three miles later, we arrived.

To me, the U.S. Consulate looked like a cross between a prison and a kindergarten. The large compound was surrounded by a simple, yet very heavy-looking, concrete wall bearing colorful murals in the style of children's crayon drawings, depicting symbols of cooperation between the U.S. and Thailand. A long line of people extended from the entrance at the street. After standing in this line for a bit, an official informed us that American citizens could proceed to a different window where there were only one or two people lined up. I reached the window and, after briefly describing my needs, was handed a telephone. When connected, the voice on the other end sounded like a machine, but was quite human. It was hard to hear because we were still on the rather noisy street. I again described our situation and asked if there was someone with whom we could meet.

"To speak with a consulate official you must have an appointment," the voice rattled off. "You must bring all of your completed paperwork to the appointment. Go to the website for instructions." I hung up the phone.

We recessed from the well-guarded doors. I hadn't expected to accomplish much on this first visit. Yet, with passports and other credentials, I really was surprised that we literally didn't get off the street. That was enough stress for the first day.

Meeting Guardian Angels

The next day, we were at the hospital to visit you, Alex and Max, and get an update from the doctor. BNH Hospital, formerly Bangkok Nursing Home, was starting to become quite familiar to us. We were really impressed. There were beautiful cascading water fountains at the front steps. Just inside the main entrance was a large, well-cooled lobby with thirty foot ceilings and a player piano that continually filled the room with elegant music, mostly familiar western melodies.

I went through the same procedure again before seeing you boys, which would become quite familiar. I put on the hospital gown and rubbed sterilizing fluid on my hands. Your conditions seemed little changed, beyond having different gowns and being in slightly different positions. The young nurse who had led me in watched as I hovered around the incubators,

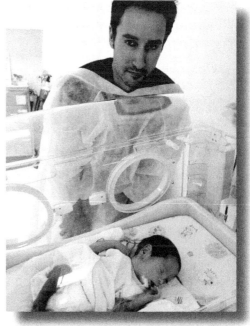

Joseph Hahle at Max's incubator.

studying every little feature I could see, and whispering to you words of encouragement. Alex, your eyes were occasionally open, and I was amazed at how dark and emotionless they seemed to be. Max, you seemed to have regurgitated your latest feeding onto your sleeping pad, which I quickly brought to the attention of the nurse. I took a few snapshots with my smart phone whenever I found a clear shot. It was magical to be there at your sides, but also frustrating. I had come thousands of miles to be with you, but was still separated from you by those walls of plastic. I knew you had a long recovery ahead, and that I would have to be patient.

We were in the waiting room anticipating a talk with the doctor after seeing you two. My mom looked across the room and noticed what appeared to be a gay couple with their two, new twins. Dad and I would have just left things as they were. Mom can't help but reach out and say "hi" to people. Several minutes later we were shaking hands with Andrew and Paul from Australia. They introduced us to their two new sons, William and Wesley, who had been born full term on Christmas Day, just three days before the two of you.

Our visit with the doctor went as expected. Then we ended up leaving the hospital with Andrew and Paul. It quickly became apparent that these guys had lots of experience with Bangkok, and that part of the world in general. Andrew was quite a talker. He kept spouting out stories and facts. He shared little pieces of knowledge that would have taken the three of us hours or even days to figure out. He taught us things like how to call America with our new cell phone, or the right way to hail a cab, which was second nature to Andrew. Better than that, they were doing the exact same thing with their set of twins we were preparing for with you, thus giving us a sneak peek at our future. These guys were really savvy about everything around us, and we needed someone just like them. So we were thrilled.

In the coming days we would meet up with them to be led around town to learn all sorts of things that were very helpful for us to know.

Within a few days, a routine began to emerge. Each day included a walk to the hospital to see you boys, an outing to some new store or other location of interest, and a new restaurant experiment or meal at home.

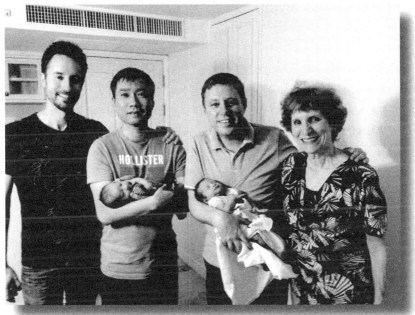

Our new friends, Paul and Andrew, holding their twins, William and Wesley.

As we walked around different parts of our neighborhood, we began occasionally noticing crowds of people in colorful shirts. Often they were blowing shrill whistles, and sometimes were led by a person shouting through a loudspeaker, although nothing that we could understand. Andrew and Paul informed us that these were the political protesters, the same we had been hearing about months ago on the news, the same the Thai Embassy officials in L.A. said would be gone by the time we made our trip. But they weren't gone.

There were even more of them. And they didn't look or sound particularly happy.

Apparently, the protests had been slowly gaining strength over the last several months. They seemed to like to congregate at major street intersections, public parks and entrances to popular shopping locations. As we ventured further out in town, it became apparent that these activists were everywhere. Occasionally we would be heading somewhere, maybe the store, and would have to push our way through a gathering of these people blowing their noisy whistles and waving Thai flags. We just kept our heads down respectfully and tried to go unnoticed.

We watched the news every day for the latest headlines. We kept asking people we met about how serious they thought the situation was, but it was hard to really get a sense. The way things were was a minor inconvenience. If it got worse, there was no telling how this could affect our plans.

Unwanted Visitors

Most people are afraid of something. It may be heights for one person, lightning for someone else. It could be earthquakes, wrinkles, rejection, aliens, death by drowning, bees. Whatever it is, each can cause someone out there to forget everything else around them and focus on the fear of that thing. This chapter might send one of you boys squirming to the exit, while the other might not understand what the big deal is. Either way, the tale must be told because it was a significant bump in the road on my way to fatherhood. In my opinion, your story simply wouldn't be complete without it.

It was our 3rd day in the apartment and, beyond the faint odor that was only really evident each time we arrived; I think we were cautiously satisfied. We were trying very hard to conserve funds because we still didn't know just how much everything would cost us by the time we returned home.

I stepped into the living/dining room after a nap and something caught my eye on the floor near the table leg. It was dark brown with a sort-of flattened-football shape. My memory thinks of it as the size of a smart phone. In reality that is a major exaggeration. Regardless, as I quickly approached, fearing the worst, the details of the thin, plastic-looking wings emerged. I began to shake my head back and forth while vocalizing a low, guttural tone. If this helps you understand my mood at that time, picture an adult's reaction to a small child who is across a room and about to pour a glass of water on the adult's laptop.

I called out with warning to my mom who wasn't far away. Before she could respond, I had crushed the dark, flat football with a blunt object. Honestly, I tend to be the type that catches a wayward insect and transitions it to the out of doors where it can go on its way. That's not easy with insects this fast. And if they get away inside the house, it can lead to a much, much bigger problem.

I would say I don't have a cockroach phobia, at least no more than I imagine the average person has. Yet I certainly don't want them *on* me. You know what they say about these pests. If you see one, it's likely there are tons more present. If there are tons present, what are the odds of having them crawling on you at night? My babies would hopefully be with us soon. What were the odds of giant cockroaches crawling on *you* at night? That thought was just not acceptable to me. Period!

We proceeded with a discussion regarding whether the roach I had squashed was a fluke that had just wandered in the front door or one of many hiding behind the wall. It was decided, since it was the only one we had seen to that point, that the former was the case.

The next day, I wandered into the living/dining room, looked toward the floor at a corner of the room, and saw another proud roach. It quickly darted back behind a large cabinet with shelves that was built into the wall. At that moment I knew we had an infestation and a real problem. We notified the apartment staff, who recommended that the unit be sprayed. They did so in short order.

The next day, I wandered into the living/dining room, looked toward the floor and saw a roach busily crossing the short, green carpet. Then I spied another one in another part of the room. A few minutes later, a little one on the wall scurried behind the dish cabinet. The management's spray hadn't killed the roaches. It had driven them out of their hiding spots into the rooms!!

That night, I got in bed to go to sleep. Laying there in the silence, I could hear delicate sounds of movement behind the wardrobe. The sound would come and go as the minutes ticked by. I turned on the bedside lamp and looked over the head of the bed towards the corner where the wardrobe stood. A large cockroach pranced out of the shadows and headed past the bed – its head over an inch from the floor as it crept. It spotted me and ran the opposite direction. I followed it. All the while it kept turning in avoidance. It was fleeing back to the wardrobe corner when I finally caught up with it and gave it a quick end with an old walking cane.

Where had he come from? Was there a hole in the wall? I eyed the wardrobe with suspicion and then heaved a corner of it out from the wall. I was stunned at what I saw. There was a doorknob, a doorframe, a whole seven foot tall door in the wall hidden behind the wardrobe! Where did this door lead?

I studied the wall and walked around to the other side. The door would have opened out into the living room. The massive cabinet, built into the wall, where I had spotted roaches earlier was covering the opening. Could this be the roach lair? I returned to my bedroom and pulled the wardrobe fully out. With dread, I opened the door and peered inside. There were no swarms of roaches or nests or eggs. There were just layers of dust, a bit of construction debris, and the back of the cabinet. Yet, the cabinet was huge. Its labyrinth of wood headed off deep into the shadows, beyond sight and beyond reach. There was no telling what was back there. Maybe there was an army of wallet sized roaches, piled up high just behind the edge of the light, waiting silently for the predator to pass without noticing. I closed the door and returned the wardrobe to its corner. It was very late, so I forced myself to sleep.

During the night I woke to a strange sensation. I was sleeping on my side when something seemed to be moving the hair on the back of my head. I lurched up from the bed. I shook out my hair and checked my clothes and white sheets for a large insect. I found nothing. Little sleep was to be had by me the rest of that night.

The next day, after a visit to the hospital, my key mission was the annihilation of our bug problem. It would end, or we would be moving. I purchased the best spray I could find and several other items. We covered up all of the food and clothes, etc. With great care I made my way through the entire unit, spraying each crack, crevice and corner. I saved a large amount of the spray for the back of the living room cabinet. I then gathered my parents for a long afternoon in the nearby park and a few errands.

Five hours later, upon our return, the odor from the chemicals was supposed to be gone, but it really wasn't. I was trying to save us from the bugs. Yet, what good would that do if fumes killed us in the process?

We found an extra window to open. The cross breeze seemed to help.

As for roaches? None yet.

I pulled the wardrobe out from the corner of my bedroom and spent half an hour carefully sealing all of the openings around and below the hidden door with packaging tape. If any roaches had survived the poison, they wouldn't be coming at me through that door. I also attached double-sided tape to the legs of the bed, so that any roach attempting to climb would get stuck. I even put roach-poison food in a corner of each room. If I was to fail in defeating the roaches, it certainly was not going to have been from a lack of trying.

I spent the next few days a little traumatized. Each time I entered a room of the apartment, I was looking to the corners, expecting to see a roach. Sleeping was difficult. I had taken precautions, yet those roaches had wings. They could always fly onto the bed. I couldn't purge the thought from my head of a big roach running up the covers and falling onto my face.

Okay! Okay! Maybe I have a *little* roach phobia! I admit it. I know there are millions of other people who can relate. My mother is one of them. She was thankful for my efforts. My dad, on the other hand, showed almost complete immunity. It is quite possible that if I had not made a complaint, he would have been oblivious to their very existence.

We saw a few roaches after I sprayed, yet they were barely moving. The fact is, the only roach we saw in the apartment from that day forward, was a dead roach. I was victorious and deeply relieved.

I felt strongly that this unfortunate experience was not a reflection on Bangkok in general or any particular establishment. That sort of thing could have happened almost anywhere in the world. We just got really unlucky that time around.

A Huge Pile of Red Tape

Days earlier, I had been gathering the required documents from the U.S. Consulate website that had to be filled out and submitted at our interview. At the same time, I signed on to schedule the interview itself. I was shocked to see that the earliest interview opportunity was five weeks away, and you, my sons, had to be physically present at the interview. I signed up immediately, of course. Then the more I thought about it, the more it seemed that five weeks might actually end up being too soon. Your premature birth and subsequent condition made it difficult to know for sure when you would be released from the hospital. One got the feeling that this tangled web of hoops might stretch on for a very long time indeed.

At least I had a nice long window of opportunity to fill out my paperwork. The necessary documents included a Consular Report of Birth Abroad and a passport application, photo required. Other documents I had to present included your Thai birth certificates with attached official English translations, copies of my contracts with the clinic and copies of official identification from the surrogate. I also had to provide my passport and samples of my pay stubs as evidence of my U.S. citizenship and at least five years of physical presence in the United States. Include two of some of these documents for two babies, and you get a pretty heavy stack of material to keep organized. The pay stubs actually had to be gathered back in the U.S. and sent to me by a friend of mine.

Each day I did some work filling out documents and gathering information. We could not afford to fail during our interview, which would require waiting for a new appointment. All of our documentation had to be perfect.

Baby Progress

About the 4th day, we met with the cardiologist who had diagnosed your heart ailment, Max. We were elated to receive the news that your condition had been overcome entirely with the use of medication. No surgery would be needed! We were all so extremely relieved and thankful. Within two days, the pediatrician was able to reduce your oxygen supplement to zero. You were breathing on your own. Another great milestone!

Since the first day, I had been noticing, Max, that your ears were a bit unusual. Don't get me wrong, just being alive and my son made you absolutely beautiful. Yet your ears were papery thin and overly convoluted. Your right ear bore an unsightly groove with no lobe running down to your face, presumably a result of your prematurity. This concerned me a bit, and I was watching. By the end of the first week, your right ear was filling in and was almost normal-looking. I can think of no example that better described your ear's progress than a deflated balloon that had slowly been filled. You were catching up quickly to Alex, who had been dreaming away day after day, absorbing milk and getting bigger.

Ever since you boys had been born, there were distinct differences in how you were developing. I suppose I expected this. Being fraternal twins, you were already genetically quite different. Your measurements, such as heart rate and weight, had been different since early in the pregnancy. I did wonder if you would tend to become more alike over time or if I would continue to notice differences throughout your lives. At the moment, it was all about celebrating each little step forward. I was so proud of both of you.

Temple Tour Day
and Crisis

We'd been in Bangkok well past a week. Up to this point, our energies were absorbed with hospital visits, consulate paperwork, and simply learning how to survive. The original plan was to arrive a few weeks before the birth. That way we would be present for that occasion and also have a chance to have some fun in one of the most popular travel destinations in the world. Your early arrival changed that whole equation. Regardless, at a week in with both of you strengthening, we began to realize that if we were going to do any touring while in Bangkok, this was our best opportunity.

My mom wanted to see elephants in the wild. We were staying in the heart of Bangkok. A trip into the remote countryside, as interesting as that sounds, would make us *way* late for our next hospital visit. So we turned our eyes back toward the city.

At the top of the tourist list in Thailand were the grand palace and temples, which happened to be just across town. We booked seats on a group van tour. A day later, we were on our way, excited to be doing something completely different.

We saw temple after temple with gold, colorful tiles, enormous elaborate paintings and Buddha. Buddha, Buddha, Buddha Buddha. And about 10,000 more Buddhas. We saw one gold Buddha which was reclining and about half the length of a football field. Another Buddha was about 11,000 pounds of solid gold. I've got complete respect for Buddhism. Yet, for me, the repetition of this religious icon was mind-boggling. If there was anything I learned that day about Buddhism, it's that apparently you could never have enough statues of Buddha!

After several individual temples, we arrived at the Grand Palace complex, a huge area surrounded by a wall that, as of this writing, has been the official residence of the Kings of Siam since 1782. The Grand Palace temples were especially large and beautiful. I actually had to purchase a cheap pair of long pants on the street before entering because my shorts didn't satisfy the palace complex's dress code. This was where everything started to unravel.

Your grandfather is not one to complain about discomfort. He grew up on a farm in the late 40's and 50's, and spent years in the remote Guyanese jungle, as a missionary. He's always been an outdoorsman and adventurer. In other words, he's a tough guy. So it was unusual to hear him say that he was feeling weak, and needed to stop and sit down.

It was a hot day. We had been walking around quite a bit. Maybe a drink of water and a rest would have him feeling better. My mom stayed with him. I agreed to continue with the tour and check back with them in 20 minutes or so.

The group only contained one other couple besides us. Somewhere along the way, that couple decided to sit down in a courtyard and take a break. We agreed to meet back with them after circling another group of temples. Suddenly, it was just me and the tour guide, which felt weird. She was leading me around, talking about the significance of this and that. I was barely paying attention. I felt like I was at a dance where everyone had disappeared except for the DJ and me.

The tour guide was rattling off some story about why a particular statue's feet had a certain number of toes, when I butted in, "You know, I think we better get back to the others." She agreed, and we headed on around with little delay.

The couple we had left in the courtyard was nowhere to be found. So we headed over to where I had left my parents and found them. Dad was worse, which was a real concern. He needed a bathroom, which nobody could find. The tour guide explained that there was an ice cream shop and bathroom back at the entrance to the complex, about a four minute walk from where we were. My dad was so weak at this point that he couldn't walk without assistance. This was something I'd never witnessed before in my life! Despite this, at *his* suggestion, I agreed to something that seems utterly unbelievable when I think about it today. I agreed to walk him to the ice cream shop, where he would wait alone until the rest of us finished the tour. In hindsight, it was ridiculous! The culture in our family dictates that when you buy something or have a special opportunity, like a temple tour, you make use of it without waste. Yet this was just plain stupid.

I put my dad's arm over my shoulder and we slowly made our way toward the ice cream shop. This was the first time I can remember physically supporting my dad. For the 37 years of my life, he was always the one we all drew strength and security from. Now, *he* was leaning on me. On our way, we passed right in front of the Grand Palace. Should we stop briefly and take a quick picture? The thought passed through my mind, but I immediately realized the absurdity of it. We reached the ice cream shop where I placed my dad at a table. He assured me he would be okay. So I returned to the tour group, as planned.

The missing couple from our group had been located, so we proceeded. Yet, the resumption of a pleasant tour wasn't going to work. Mom and I couldn't stop thinking about my dad. After viewing a couple of ancient thrones, we abandoned the tour for the last time to reunite with my father.

He was still conscious at the ice cream shop, barely. He told us he had nearly fainted while crouching in the restroom, which was little more than a hole in the floor. We had to prop him on both sides a bit later, as the tour group reboarded the van, or he would have fallen. Back at our rented Bangkok home, we made sure he drank some water and put him straight to bed. Hopefully, he would be feeling better the next day.

As it was still early afternoon, I went on my own to the hospital to visit you boys. To my delight I found you, Alex, were no longer in an incubator. You were out on your own on a little plastic tray, just like all the other babies. I was told that it might be around two more weeks before you'd be able to come home. You sure were looking more ready.

Max, you were looking great too. You were often moving around and stretching your arms. Alex had gained 30 grams that day, and you grew 37.

With you boys improving and likely to come home in the near future, I began to think about how crucial it was that the rest of us stay healthy. We didn't know for sure what had caused my dad to feel ill. If it was transmittable, we couldn't afford to expose you infants to that disease. There was also a serious logistical threat. Two adults might be able to care for two infants and a sick adult. Yet, if two adults were sick, especially if one or more needed to be hospitalized, there wouldn't be enough adults left to care for all. What would we do? This seemed like another potential disaster waiting to happen.

Dad's Hospitalization

The next day we were expecting Dad to be better. He wasn't!

About midway through the day, he was weaker with a headache, nausea, and a 104-degree temperature that seemed to be rising! Not surprisingly, my dad was still not sure that the hospital was necessary. Yet, the time for waiting and frugality had passed.

Normally, we could make the walk to the hospital in 10 minutes. In his condition, even with our help, this wasn't an option. Unfortunately, we had not yet mastered the art of cab hailing. *If* we managed to call the hospital, we probably wouldn't be able to correctly communicate what we needed or the apartment's address, which was a confusing several sentences long. Also, the apartment staff spoke so little English that it was hard getting across to them what our situation was. We had a real dilemma.

Thankfully, after some trouble, I did manage to get someone at the front desk to call for a cab. We struggled to get Dad to the street and into the car. Then we were headed for the hospital. The cab driver was confused about where we needed to go. Some of the streets had been blocked to certain turns because of rush hour. When a traffic jam had us going nowhere, on a road actually leading us away from the hospital, we were almost ready to get out and start walking!

We got the traffic and directional issues straightened out. After what seemed like an eternity, we reached the emergency room. Dad was given an IV. His temperature was dropping, so we felt like we could finally breathe a sigh of relief.

The doctor suspected e-coli poisoning. After some tests, Dad was given antibiotics. He spent the night at the hospital, just a minute's walk from you boys down the hall. Mom and I now had three people to visit. The hospital was winning the tug of war battle.

It was the following afternoon when we took Dad home. Blame was placed on gastroenteritis, a bacterial infection of the digestive tract, causing severe diarrhea, nausea and dangerous dehydration. We suspected tainted street food. We had been eating from a few of the local carts now and then when convenient. In truth, we did not know where the bug originated.

A Day in Bangkok

On Sunday, after church, we visited you boys.

Max, you were out of your incubator. I got to hold you and Alex for about 5 minutes each. Then, both of you were wheeled around to the main viewing window where Mom and Dad got to see you. We noticed, Max, that your fingernails were sharp, pointed and would probably need to be trimmed soon. Both of you seemed to be improving in color each day. Up to that time, you both had spells of considerable rosiness, especially in your faces. Our friend, Andrew, suspected that you might

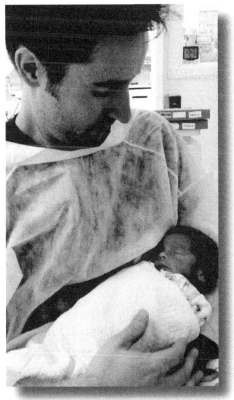

Joseph Hahle holding Alexander Hahle.

actually turn out to be gingers, which is a nickname for people with pale, freckled skin and red hair. I was pretty sure that wasn't the case. The doctor said it would likely be several more days before you would be able to suck milk from a bottle.

That afternoon, we visited the large Lumphini Park several blocks away. The protests were in full swing. We had to pass through a large area at the entrance of the park that was filled with tents, speakers and other equipment – all related to the movement. There had been a few new reports of violence in the city. As the protests drew more attention, areas they most frequented were beginning to draw street vendors and other groups of people who wanted to take advantage of the business opportunities. This was just drawing in more people, and congestion was starting to become a serious issue.

I don't remember seeing any squirrels in the park. We *were* amazed to see a number of komodo dragons running free, one of them at least four feet long. We lay in the grass on a provided mat during a Bangkok symphony concert at one of the outdoor entertainment areas, an experience that was quite enjoyable.

On our way home, we pushed through more activists and stopped at the mall at a nice Indian restaurant, that had become a favorite. The waiter described the chicken vindaloo as medium to medium hot in spiciness. I had already had the regular chicken curry another evening, which was mild. So I figured I'd live a little and go for it. I think I did a pretty good job of masking the excruciating pain that followed. The food was extremely hot, while so good that I couldn't bring myself to stop eating.

That night, around 12:30 a.m., the vindaloo came back to haunt my gut. Another whole bottle of water and two Mylanta® tablets from Mom got me through the night. At this point I resolved I'd had my spicy meal for the trip. Milk was my dear friend once again.

The Bangkok Alley Shortcut

The days continued to pass, with our Bangkok home becoming ever more familiar. Mom was trying harder to assert her special influence on the apartment. She had removed many of the pre-hung wall hangings that she either didn't care for or thought were dusty. She ended up putting most of them right back because they were hiding nail holes or other unsightly wall blemishes of one kind or another.

Jeanie Hahle in the living room of our apartment in Bangkok.

There was a little end table just outside our front door that held an ashtray that was used, apparently quite frequently, by any of the tenants on that floor. Mom was radically anti-smoking so I should have figured she would do something special with the tray. I knew she would never submit to emptying the tray into a trashcan where she might possibly smell it. I learned some time much later that Mom had been heaving the ashes over the plants at a street overlook a few steps away. One couldn't see beyond the plants. After the toss, the ashes would be gone and she could pretend they never existed. That overlook led straight to the side street two floors down. It was hard to say just where the food vendors were setting up day to day. Since then, I've wondered if any bowl of noodles or Thai iced tea was ever christened with a cloud of Mom's vanishing cigarette ashes.

I cut my dad's hair one night. The funniest part probably came with my mom and me arguing about how to arrange the chair for him to sit on. I've been cutting my own hair for many years, so it wasn't that big a deal. Nonetheless, I'd never live down having my father walking around Bangkok with a huge chunk of hair errantly missing from the side of his head. So I was relieved when he looked in the mirror and enthusiastically approved the finished job.

We continued to make a daily pilgrimage to the hospital to spend some time with you. We'd have lunch somewhere, pick up a few groceries or baby care items, and try to find some other little outing of intrigue to fill the rest of the afternoon. On one particular day, we caught a cab to the nearby library, which ended up being closed. So we devised a strategy for walking to the nearest sky train (elevated public transit system), to take us across the nearby Chao Phraya River to see what we could see. The sky train was several blocks away to the south. We were having trouble finding a single street that led in that direction.

We came upon this nicely maintained alley leading straight south and I thought, "This should work". So we made the turn and started walking.

All of the streets we had been on up to that point were packed with traffic, noise, motorcycles, strange smells, and hordes of people. It was quite refreshing to be on a roadway that was clean, quiet and curiously did not include a single bit of traffic.

We kept walking. A couple minutes in, I noticed the alley narrowing slightly ahead. Everything looked secure, so no worry. The sound of the city faded behind us as we walked. A bit later, the road turned into something more like a crumbly walkway with the condition of the property on either side going downhill. There wasn't a person in sight, which felt disconcerting. Yet, I could still see way ahead. We were so far in, we couldn't turn back now.

I kept telling myself, "Stay the course. Any moment now, a nice, full-sized street with cars and people and noises and smells will come into view."

Further we penetrated into the unknown. I peeked back at my dad who gave me a reassuring nod. The narrow walkway between the buildings shrunk down again to maybe four-feet wide and now bore a crudely fashioned tarp roof. I began seeing things I just shouldn't be seeing: kitchen counters, pet feeding dishes, laundry I almost had to duck to get around, a tiny child by himself.

"Onward! The road must be ahead!"

We passed a bench where three, crude-looking men were seated. They watched with confused interest as we came and passed by.

"Nothing to see here!" I said in my head. "We're just passing through. We're on our way to the street ahead!"

We continued on a bit further. In my mind I was nearing defeat. Another 20 steps would probably lead us through someone's bathroom. That thought was just too much to bear. We passed a couple women with that same confused expression on their faces. Finally, we stopped. One of those women was talking with my mom and explained our fate fully when I heard three simple words, "No way out." The woman gave a little giggle and sweet smile as we all said a soft, and in my case, embarrassed, "thank you."

On our way out, we passed the same crude-looking, three men, who watched us come and go just as intently as they had before. Had they seen three, clean-cut, camera-bearing, falsely-confident, white tourists march through their back patio, only to march right back the opposite direction, head in hand, before? Or were we really just the most ridiculous people to have ever walked down that particular alley? We made it back past the cat bowls, the laundry, the kitchen counters and the tiny child. We were in the clear!

My mom doesn't really do sarcasm. Yet, you might not have believed that if you had heard her state, "Well, Joe, that was really interesting!"

Dreaded Bath Lessons

Alex and Max, a little less than three weeks since the birth, you were free of feeding tubes and well ahead of your recovery schedule! Before the hospital would let us take you home, we had to demonstrate our ability to meet your basic needs. You each had to swallow 30 milliliters of milk within 30 minutes. The time limit was present mostly because that's about as long as a newborn could stay awake before sleeping an hour and a half before the next feeding. We also had to show that we could bathe you. Everything was focused on me, because I am your actual parent.

I had been going to a back room of the NICU to attempt feedings and get bathing lessons. I use the word "attempt" because at this premature stage, you don't just stick the bottle in the baby's mouth and hold it while he sucks. The sucking reflex had not fully developed. This means it could be past the prescribed feeding time with a full serving of milk, and you would just hold the nipple in your mouth looking up at me, as if to say "now what?" There were a variety of little techniques the nurses used to encourage the baby to suck the bottle. There were different positions in which to hold the baby, little motions on the bottle, and tapping on the bottle with a fingernail. I have to admit, the nurses were good at this. It wasn't easy. The first couple times I tried bore zero success.

Then there were the bath lessons. I hated this. Remember, you babies were small enough for your entire bodies to fit

115

between the palm of my hand and elbow. Your necks and limbs were so thin and fragile-looking, it seemed like one errant movement could seriously injure you. It didn't help that the moment you touched the water, you would scream. That torture would last until you were dry and back in your swaddle.

The first time I went in for the bathing, I just watched as the nurse confidently and quickly went about a task she did numerous times a day. When it was my turn, of course, I went *slowly*. It didn't seem slow to me because every movement seemed so death defying. I didn't want to make any mistakes! One nurse, who often coached me, gave me a particularly hard time. I would be moving as fast as I thought I could, and this person would stand four feet away with folded arms, tapping her toe and giving me a look like I was inconveniencing everyone. I don't think she was evil. I just think she was a little young and insensitive. I also suppose she wanted to encourage me to move with a little more confidence for my own good. I wasn't about to scold her for being pushy. This girl was closely caring for you babies whenever we weren't there, so I certainly didn't want to get on her bad side!

After the second uncomfortable episode with this nurse, I knew I had to do something. So I went shopping with my parents and bought a baby-sized, teddy bear wearing overalls to practice on. It was the closest thing to a life-size, baby doll I could find. We went back to the apartment where I spent a chunk of the evening pretending to bath the teddy bear. I went through all of the steps and motions in detail: undressing the teddy, cleaning its naval with a sterile Q-tip®, gently washing its non-existent hair, cleaning each nostril and ear, and its mouth, drying, re-diapering, clothing, and swaddling. Then I would do it all over again. I think my parents thought it was a little silly. They had not been dealing with that nurse!

The next day, I went to my bathing lesson. I wasn't a pro, and she wasn't stunned at my progress. Yet, I was feeling better about *myself* and I did get by with fewer corrections. I can remember washing your hair one day, Alex, as you cried with the nurse giving me some glares and looking at her watch. I started softly singing a nursery rhyme to soothe you, but changed the words to describe the insensitivity of the nurse. She was the only one close enough to hear. I was basically mumbling, and she spoke little English, so I knew she wouldn't be able to understand what I was saying. "Hush little baby don't say a word, she's the meanest nurse that you e-ver heard."

I got through a few lines of gentle, poorly worded criticism like this, and was feeling quite warm and fuzzy. She was looking on with considerable curiosity. "I want know what you say." She told me. I smiled.

"It's just an old baby song," I replied. Despite the stress she

Joseph Hahle holding Max and Alex.

gave me, I believe this nurse actually cared deeply for you babies. When we would visit the hospital at random times, it often seemed to be her that had either of the two of you slung at her waist.

BNH was a great hospital. I would go back there in a second.

117

A Meal
at the Top of the World

I have a great friend who is deeply afraid of heights. We like to joke that he can't make it past the second step on a ladder without looking down in panic. That's a small exaggeration. We hike together regularly. It is common practice for him to stop on a trail, despite my pleas, and let me continue alone to a summit, sometimes just a stone's throw away. *I'm* not particularly afraid of heights or so I thought before this day.

We were anticipating the release of at least one of you from the hospital in the next several days, and figured this was the right time to get out and do something special. Our Australian friends, Andrew and Paul, had recommended a fancy restaurant just a twenty minute walk from our apartment. We are the type of people that rarely spend more than $30 on a special occasion meal, but once in a great while, especially when a rare opportunity arose, it was important to splurge. What made this restaurant exceptional was that it was on the top roof of a building that was 61 stories tall and a truly unsettling maybe 35 *feet* wide!

The Banyan Tree building, Bangkok.

We arrived at the building, the Banyan Tree hotel. An elevator whisked us to what we thought was the top floor. We were a bit early for dinner, so beyond the occasional hotel clerk, we were basically exploring on our own. It's one thing to go up high into a skyscraper and look out through a window at the tiny, ant-like people on the ground far below. It's quite another thing for that plane-like view to reveal itself on one side *and* the other simultaneously. It gave me the immediate feeling I had wandered into a dangerous place where I really wasn't supposed to be.

We stepped delicately into the room lined with glowing panes of glass flowing with water. A hostess casually directed us toward a nearby stairway. I was already feeling unsure. Then I was climbing an elaborate spiral stairway that was taking us further *up*. It felt like an exotic mansion that must be hanging beneath a blimp. If this were a James Bond movie, the next clerk would politely direct me through a door leading to the open sky where I would fall to my doom.

We reached the top of the long spiral stairway and approached an opening to an outside veranda that overlooked the city – a fantastic view! Now, another clerk was directing me up again. This stairway was on the outside of the building. Just over the left handrail, it was a 640-foot straight drop to the ground below. I looked behind me at my mother who looked like she might not be breathing. My dad was smiling and clearly very entertained. At the top of this stairway, our restaurant, appropriately named *The Vertigo*, finally came into view. I do believe if the staff greeting us had not been so confident and well dressed, I might not have been able to stay due to the height-inspired feeling of dread I was experiencing. Soon, we were taken to our table and a most enjoyable and simply sensational evening began.

The sun was setting, and the skyscraper encrusted landscape of Bangkok shot into the sky all around us. Our meals were served on silver platters with elaborate covers. The presentation was awesome. The staff counted down, "three, two, one," then raised the covers in unison to reveal the entrees, which were as wonderful and delectable as the atmosphere.

After the meal, there was plenty of time to wander around and take in the sights. A sharp eye could identify different protest encampments around town that had turned into little "towns". Far below and directly in view, was BNH hospital where you, Alexander and Maximus, continued to gain strength. You couldn't be with us that time. Maybe someday I would be able to bring you to that amazing place and show you how I looked down from above and prayed for your long-awaited homecoming. In a way, you had taken us there. If it were not for you, we never would have had that experience.

The view from the top of the Banyan Tree building in Bangkok.

The Day You Came Home

It had been almost one month since you were born. I had demonstrated adequate baby bathing skills, you boys were drinking your prescribed quota of milk from a bottle, and each of you had exceeded the target weight. The doctor wanted your lungs to strengthen a bit more, Max. But it was time for you, Alexander, to come home. I was very excited and a bit nervous. We had discussed our plan for baby transport and at-home care quite a lot. It was all theory until the real, breathing, squirming life was there in our hands.

We met with the doctor one more time for her final go-ahead. The nurses had just finished bathing both of you boys. They had a special way of swaddling babies on the day they would go home. A little piece of the cloth would stick out over the head, like a cap or visor, to help protect the face from the sun.

We carefully secured you, Alex, in your mobile car seat, which we had chosen as the way we would be carrying you guys around. Your body was still so small that the only way we could use the straps was to put your feet where you would normally sit. Eventually we got you neatly secured, and tied a very thin, breathable scarf over the entire outfit to hide you, and protect you from the city air.

A number of the nurses who had cared for you came out to see you off. It was clear they had developed an attachment for both of you and were sad to see you, Alex, leaving. To this day, I wish we had taken a picture of all of them at that moment. Our thoughts were so focused on your safe transport that we could think of little else.

The car seat had a long handle that arced over the top, which made it easy for two people to walk on either side and carry some of the weight simultaneously. My dad and I took this responsibility as we exited the hospital. After weeks with both of you immobile and entirely dependent on the hospital, it felt extremely odd to be carrying you out – almost like we were stealing you.

I kept thinking someone would stop us and say, "Hey! Where are you taking that baby? You can't do that!" No one did.

Alex, you were fast asleep, but actually having the ride of your life. We made our way down the occasionally narrow sidewalks bustling with people and street vendors. There weren't any protest sites on this path, thankfully. Traffic was quite noisy, as always, and we had a few streets to cross that required special alertness and timing. Nobody we passed could have imagined our situation. This was a single, gay American and his reverend father carrying their newborn son / grandson, born to a surrogate, for the first time into uncharted territory –

Dennis and Joseph Hahle carrying Alex.

the first steps into the journey of this new life.

I was relieved to reach the apartment. It was time to see if all our preparations would work out. We had brought two miniature travel cribs, each about two and a half feet long which sat easily on a bed or table. Alex, you were transferred into one of these immediately where you continued sleeping.

The small kitchen counter was reorganized into a makeshift bathing and dressing zone. We had lots of milk bottles and diapers along with all of the accessories and items recommended for baby care. Mom had been through this with all of us kids 37 years earlier. She was rusty, but had a pretty good idea of what she was doing.

You slept and slept. Every few minutes you would squirm around a little bit and make some gurgling sounds. Every two hours you needed milk and, from time to time, a diaper change. It all seemed to go according to plan.

Then, came the night. We knew that newborns required feeding every two hours, *including* during the night. So we discussed our options and devised a shift schedule. I would take responsibility for Alex during the first night shift from 9 p.m. to 3 a.m., during which my parents would have uninterrupted sleep. Then, you would be transferred to their room until 8 a.m.

Mom and Dad went to bed. My shift started out easy enough. I tend to be a night owl anyway. So I was sort-of excited to be taking charge for a while. Alex, a couple hours later, you were due for your next feeding. It's amazing how clockwork babies' stomachs are. Ten minutes before the appointed time, you would begin to increase your squirming and gurgling. Five minutes before, you would start to let out some soft, short cries. When the two hours was fully up, more faithfully than a geyser in Yellowstone, you would be in a state of full continuous sobs. Of course, I'd try to be ready ahead of time, so you wouldn't need to cry.

We were using a special, extra-calorie formula that the hospital had provided. We had brought a small bottle-warming machine from home. It took four or five minutes to mix the formula and get it warmed up. If I started during your first hints of hunger, I could usually get the bottle to you before the full-on crying. That feeding went just fine. When you were through, I re-tucked your swaddle, and gently placed you back in the mini-crib that was sitting on my bed. But this time, within 20 minutes, you were crying again. I checked your diaper. It was a little wet, so I went ahead and changed it. As soon as you were back in the crib, you resumed the crying. I considered your coverings. Were you too cold? Too hot? Neither seemed to be the case. So I picked you up and gently rocked you, which you usually found calming. The crying went on.

I knew that babies were designed to cry to get the attention of their caretaker, usually when they are uncomfortable for some reason. I learned quickly that when they are really going, this crying isn't pleasant. Rather, it is specially designed to be painful to hear – to grate at a person's soul to encourage them to take notice and action. So I was becoming pretty highly stressed. This was my first time caring for my new child as a single dad. It was very important to me to prove I was up for this challenge. For this reason I kept the door to my bedroom and parent's room fully shut, hoping that they would not be disturbed and tempted to come to give assistance.

The crying persisted. I offered you more milk. You wouldn't take it. I sang to you, but you were not impressed. Lights on, lights off – didn't seem to matter. I rocked you a bit more aggressively. Then you seemed to be screaming all the louder.

I thought to myself, "Please, Alex! Give your dad a little help here! I'm doing the best I can!" You offered no mercy. It wasn't even midnight, and I was nearing the end of what I could handle. My back started to ache. You weighed little more than a bottle of wine. Yet somehow, through all the rocking, bending over and stress, I was really starting to hurt. I began to picture my life going forward. I had sacrificed all of my time: my projects, my social life, my career, my peace, my physical comfort. They had all been superseded. I would grow old and hunched over with this miserable, screaming baby in my arms. My life was over. I'm exaggerating just a bit, but this really was the essence of the emotion I was feeling at that moment.

Then a knock came at my bedroom door, and my mom entered. "Hey," she said with a sleepy look of concern. "You don't have to do this alone." She took you out of my weary arms. "Let us take him for a while."

I followed her back to their room carrying the mini-crib, updated her on all of the things I had done to try to satisfy you, returned to my room, and crashed. I was so fatigued; I passed out and didn't see any of you again until mid-morning.

Around 9 a.m. I walked into the dining room where Mom and Dad were eating breakfast. Alex, you were asleep in the crib.

"Did you guys get any sleep?" I asked.

"Oh yes." said Mom. I was confused.

"He didn't keep you up??"

"We didn't really have any trouble with him," she said casually. Now I was dumbfounded and a little irritated. What had I done wrong? I used every trick in the book without success. Mom acted like she put you in the crib, turned out the light, and you slept like an angel. Factually, I knew she had been up for the required feedings, but otherwise, she reported no anomalies. Maybe it just took a woman's touch? After all, you babies had been cared for almost exclusively by women ever since you had been born. Whatever it was, it remains a mystery. I was so thankful to have my parents with me.

There's nothing that can prepare a person for baby care like taking care of a baby. Within a few days, taking care of Alex still wasn't a snap, but I had become much more comfortable with it. The biggest problem I had: sleeping. Alex wouldn't be quiet. Even as he slept he would squirm and grunt, squirm and coo, squirm and gurgle. One of the nicknames we had for Alex was

"Mockingbird" because of all of the distinctly different little sounds he would make.

It was hard to tell if a particular squirm and gurgle indicated a dirty diaper, that he had wiggled out of his blanket and needed to be re-covered, that he was getting hungry, having trouble breathing, or possibly nothing at all. I think, because of how seriously I took the responsibility, I just couldn't clear my mind and sleep. Whenever I did finally pass out, he would start crying because it was already another feeding time. We didn't feel comfortable putting him in a separate room because of his prematurity. So if I had the baby shift, that gurgling baby was lying right beside me in his mini-crib. Mom and Dad seemed to be much better at isolating their thoughts and sleeping.

There were still no answers regarding that rough first night. Yet, I had learned a few simple things that had made things much easier. The most important rule was to keep the baby well fed. If his tummy was full and he was swaddled, he was very unlikely to cry. That said, the feeding could be overdone. Every now and then we would be especially proud of a seemingly very successful feeding, only to have all of the milk spit back out on our lap because it was just too much. Of course, he needed to be clean. We bathed him twice a day. Diaper changes were regular. The rest of my improvement seemed to be about nuance and conditioning – getting a good feel for what Alex needed and when, and just getting accustomed to the whole experience.

Max, you came home from the hospital four days after Alex, exactly one month after the birth. This time it was just me and Mom with you. Dad stayed home to watch after Alex. We had not planned the separate homecomings, but it ended up being a very good thing. We had found a groove with Alex. Now, we were ready to handle both of you together without getting overwhelmed.

After all was said and done at the hospital, I think we had paid BNH around $17,000 for their services, most of that for extended care of you babies after the birth. This was a lot of money. The good news: it was far less than we had feared after our first talk with the doctor.

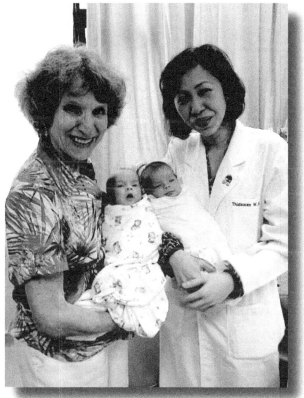

Max and Alex being held by Jeanie Hahle and their pediatrician from BNH hospital.

The Big U.S. Consulate Interview

We had been waiting five weeks for our U.S. Consulate interview. Our moment of truth had finally come. Our dear friends and mentors, Andrew and Paul, had completed their processing and had already caught a plane back home to Australia. We were on our own. We could not afford to make any mistakes. A single failing at the consulate could delay us for weeks.

The consulate website was very particular about who and what would be allowed in. No electronics were allowed. Anything else was to be in a transparent container.

Our clinic had informed us that it could make things go much more smoothly if the surrogate mother was present at the consulate appointment. We made those arrangements, agreeing to a reasonable day rate for the surrogate and a provided translator, who happened to be our primary case worker.

After a ride on the sky train and a long walk carrying you twins in your car seats, we arrived at the consulate sweaty and with very sore shoulders. The situation was stressful from all angles. First, we were far from the safety of our apartment for an unpredictable length of time with two premature infants that were just strong enough to be out of the hospital. Second, I had been detailing paperwork and studying rules for weeks, but just what would happen beyond those heavy walls was still a complete mystery. Add to that that my surrogate and translator were not at the prescribed location at the agreed upon time, and the situation felt thoroughly uncomfortable.

I can't remember how long we waited at the entrance. It was long enough for me to get good and worried about my surrogate not being present. Just as we passed through the front door, our case worker from the clinic arrived and was concerned that the surrogate was not there.

We passed awkwardly through a complex security processing area. That was when I realized that the consulate was not a building. It was more like a fortified political zone. We were only in the entry building. Soon we were directed ahead and back outside, following signs that directed us toward a completely separate group of structures. One thing that sticks with me about the consulate was the lines of people. Both outside the building and inside, people were being sorted and lined up to wait only to be sorted and lined up again, to be sorted and lined up again for various things.

We were herded into a small waiting room with a few other people and several, closed, service windows to one side. That is where our biggest wait occurred. You babies were getting restless. We had to get you out of your car seats from time to time for a feeding or a trip to the bathroom for a change.

I was reviewing my documents when an uncomfortable situation from the past week revisited my mind. One errand we had to run regarding the documentation was for official photographs of both of you for your passport applications. The photos had to comply exactly with consulate rules or they would be rejected, and would have to be re-taken. For this reason, it was highly recommended that professionals prepare them. We located a shop near our apartment that did this and headed over. It would not have been too difficult, but the consulate website clearly stated that passport photos had to be taken with eyes open. I was about to discover how extremely difficult it was to get premature infants to open their eyes at a desired moment. We wrestled with you boys for 20 minutes straight, trying every trick we could think of to get you to open your eyes long enough to photograph you that way. It wasn't happening. Milk, diaper changes, dancing, singing, loud and strange noises, ice cubes on the lips, darkness, physical manipulation, nothing worked!! It was really quite embarrassing and exasperating.

Curiously, despite all of this harassment, you were basically peaceful and asleep. Finally, randomly and without any known stimulant, each of you did open your eyes just enough and just long enough to get the crucial shot. The photographers had probably taken 70 or 80 photos of each of you before this magical feat was achieved. We were all so thankful. It was at least a week later when I happened upon an obscure line of text on the consulate website that said the open-eye rule for passport applications *did not apply to infants*. My mouth hung open as I slowly sunk low into my chair in the apartment and informed my parents of the mix-up. At least we would have the rare privilege of owning baby passport photos with eyes open.

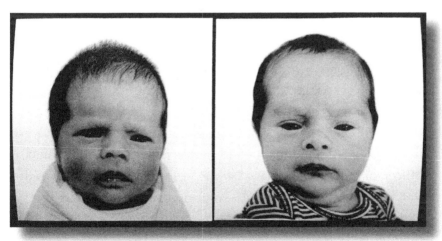

Passport photos from left to right: Alexander, Maximus.

Finally, one of the service windows opened up and people approached the station in the order they had entered the room. When we got to the window, the man heard the brief version of our story and sent us to a different part of the building to – you guessed it – line up and wait.

We had probably been at the consulate for two and a half hours. It felt like we must be getting close to the person we had come to see. Naïve, I know, but when I pictured in my mind what an interview at the U.S. consulate would be like, I saw a large, dimly lit, shadowy, quiet, private office with a distinguished consulate officer sitting behind an enormous wooden desk. We would respectfully tell him our touching story, present a few, official-looking documents, then he would wisely and understandingly sign the approval for our passage. Instead we were moved into a tiny, boxy, metal room with a stiff, flat bench. It felt like a prison cell. An ancient looking metal fan whirred above us. The room didn't seem to be temperature controlled. A small, barred, service window was at the far end of the room. After more waiting, a man approached the window and asked for my documents, which I nervously presented. He took them, one at a time, and made copies. This took a long time, as there were many documents. When he finished, I was expecting him to begin the interview. Instead it was, "Please wait for the consular officer."

At that moment, the door to the "cell" opened and in stepped Ponsai, the boys' surrogate mother. She was just in time!

The service window opened for the last time. The consular officer, at long last, appeared in the flesh. Ironically, this was the first person we had seen since entering the U.S. consulate that looked plausibly American. The sound of her voice bolstered that impression.

After briefly reviewing my documents, she began the interview. Most of her questions were aimed at revealing the story of the surrogacy and confirming my U.S. citizenship. The interview hit a brief snag when she learned of my birth in South America. Remember, my parents had all three of their children when serving as Christian missionaries in the small country of Guyana. Thankfully, Mom and Dad were present to speak on the matter themselves, with passports. The officer could tell fairly quickly my parents were plainly American.

Next, the officer asked to speak privately with Ponsai. Despite the fact that she had already signed a document with the clinic relinquishing her rights to the babies, in order to avoid confusion, the consulate welcomed surrogates to freely describe their experience, and express their agreement with the before mentioned document. There was also a section of the Consulate Report of Birth Abroad that a surrogate would sign to officially terminate her rights, which Ponsai did immediately.

The final order of business was the DNA test, to prove my biological connection to you, my sons, and qualify you for passports. This test had to be ordered by the consulate at this stage of the proceeding. The consular officer looked at us with sobriety and said, "The DNA test and passport application can take between four and eight weeks to complete."

Wow! That was tough news to hear when we'd already been away from home and work over five weeks, and struggling to care for two delicate babies. I questioned the officer how it could take four to eight weeks to complete a DNA test and passport application. Her well-rehearsed answer described the disappointing details. The consulate would provide a list of all of the approved testing facilities – all of which were located in the United States, on the other side of the planet. Once we chose a facility and ordered the test, that facility would send a new testing kit from their lab to the U.S. consulate in Bangkok. Next, the consulate would schedule a time for me to go in, and have samples taken of my babies' DNA and my DNA. This would be done by wiping a cotton swab inside our mouths. The consulate scheduled groups of parents to come in for testing, and might wait for *weeks* to schedule the test until there were enough families available to complete a group. Once the samples were received, the consulate would send the kit back to the testing facility, which would take another few days. *If* the testing facility did not have a backlog of orders, it might be able to generate results in only a couple of days. Only after confirming receipt of the DNA test results, assuming the test for paternity was positive, would the consulate begin processing the babies' applications for passports, which could take another *three weeks*. At each new turn, unexpected delay could occur.

Our interview at the U.S. consulate was finished. It was an ordeal, and left us with a lot of new homework. Thankfully, we had made it through an incredibly important hoop this day, which got us one solid step closer to going home.

A Near Death Experience

We had been at our Bangkok home from our consulate interview only long enough to eat a meal at a restaurant, which was around the corner from our apartment. Afterwards, Dad said he was a bit sleepy and laid down for a long nap.

Later in the afternoon, it was clear Dad wasn't feeling right again. He was still in bed – something he never did more than 35 or 40 minutes during the middle of the day. Mom came from their bedroom and told me that Dad was feeling drained. We weren't about to rush off to the hospital again just because he was tired.

Soon I started hearing the sound of vomiting coming from the back room. I started to really worry. Were we headed down the same path as we were during our temple tour? A couple hours passed during which I was studying some consulate documents and hoping Dad would show signs of improvement. I knew he had moved from the bedroom into the bathroom. When I heard the shower come on, it suggested to me that he was feeling stronger and able to clean up a bit.

I was sitting on the sofa feeding Alex when I heard my mom shout from the bathroom, "Joe! Help!"

She didn't need to say more. The tone of her voice told me this was a crisis. By reflex I stood up, hurriedly placed Alex on the sofa, and ran for the bathroom. Dad was standing in the shower, clenching the water pipes in front of him. Mom was up against him holding on.

"He's going down! Help!" she cried.

I ran up just as he collapsed backwards and grabbed on before his head struck the porcelain. The rest of his body hit the tub with a thud.

"What happened to him?" I yelled.

My mom replied, "He was fainting and couldn't hold on! Dennis? Den?"

Dad was not responding. My arm was still behind his neck, propping up his head as we shook him gently in desperation.

"Den? Dennis!" she continued.

I'd never seen my father in such a state. He was naked and his entire body was limp. His extra-wide-open eyes were bloodshot and seemed to be bulging out of their sockets as he stared straight into the wall, emotionless. The image was like that of a fish, pulled from the ice box, about to be cleaned.

This was my hero – the man who had been the symbol of strength and courage and wisdom and security in my life from the beginning – who had taught me many of the most important things I knew. I thought to myself, "I have come on this journey to get my newborn children. And now, my father, who I brought with me, will die here in Bangkok. After the farm in Nebraska, years of ministry in South America, a family and career, a million lives touched, and seeing his new grandsons in the hospital, *this bathtub* is where his story will end."

"Dad?" I spoke with intensity. "Dad?" Nothing from my father. "Dad, can you hear me? Say something!"

"I hear you." He uttered.

"Are you ok??"

"I'm ok. I just got a little dizzy." My dad was finally showing signs of life. His eyes sunk back into his head.

My mom and I were frightened. We kept him in the bathtub a few minutes and made him drink some water before carefully moving him back to the bed. Obviously, we were headed back to the hospital. This time the apartment staff understood what I needed a little faster than the time before. I went with Dad alone, and Mom stayed behind with you babies.

We went through the same drill at the hospital we had experienced the first time around. I had to go to the waiting room, where I sat for a long time. I was exhausted and feeling a bit defeated and insecure. You, my sons, were with us now. Our resources were spread thin. If Mom had been ill, there would have been no one left to stay home with the two of you!

Dad was being wheeled up to a room. The doctor gave me an update, speaking to me in a different tone from my dad's first incident and with deep concern in his eyes. Apparently, Dad's blood pressure had dropped dangerously low. We will never know just how serious his condition was, but I believe he could have been close to death.

Dad stayed in the hospital longer this time. Yet, the antibiotics and rehydration did eventually turn him around. Soon enough, he was able to return to the apartment with us.

The severity of his second infection and how quickly it set on was alarming. This was no longer a typical case of tourist dysentery. Dad was setting a pattern of repeated attacks that were getting worse. We had to assume that the next attack could kill him. We needed to leave. Yet, you were not physically or legally ready to travel. Putting Dad on a plane back to America didn't seem possible, because if Mom or I got sick next, we would absolutely require his help.

To make matters worse, the political protests continued to strengthen. The movement leaders had set a date in the near future when they aimed to halt all productivity in the city. They dubbed the demonstration, "Shutdown Bangkok Day". Our need to complete the process of documenting you kids, so we could get home, was more urgent than ever.

Emergency Passports

About a week passed before the U.S. consulate took DNA samples from me and the two of you, Alex and Max. Then, all we could do was wait. All the while, my mom and I were guarding my dad from eating anything suspicious. He wasn't paying as much attention, so we had to keep our eyes open. Any and all forms of street food were completely banished from the menu. If a waiter errantly brought a drink already containing ice, we had it poured out and replaced on the spot.

One day I woke to the sound of my alarm at 4 a.m. Despite the stresses surrounding us, I was determined to watch my favorite football team, the Denver Broncos, play in the Super Bowl, live. The only way to accomplish this was to get up very early to head across town to a sports bar that had advertised presentation of the game. As I walked past notable intersections on my way, I was shocked to see newly-fashioned, sand-bag walls surrounding military equipment. The "Shutdown Bangkok" demonstration was approaching, and the Thai military was apparently taking it very seriously. It was so early in the day that nobody was on the streets yet. I casually skirted around the sand bag rings and made it to the game, which ended up being an embarrassing annihilation of my precious Broncos.

On the day of the actual demonstration, we laid low. We had gathered enough food, formula and other supplies to be okay for a while. The plan was to stay in the apartment the whole day, watch the news, and avoid any possible violence in the streets. No one could tell how serious this would be. The military presence I had seen gathering suggested that a civil war could ignite at any time.

Thankfully, our apartment faced a street that was not a major gathering zone for protesters. Had we been around the block facing the mall and park, it would have been a whole other story. We wouldn't be able to see much from where we were. That was the way we wanted it. The eerie calm suggested a "tornado" was coming. This wasn't a time for curiosity. It was time to be neatly sealed in a storm shelter where, most importantly, you boys would be protected. Noise from the window increased as the day heated up. We listened and peeked out cautiously. Vehicles and motorcycles passed in the street, honking their horns and waving flags at various moments during the day. The news showed images of huge gatherings of marching protesters.

Thankfully, there was no crackdown by the military, yet. Before the day was over, the activists were already talking about the next, bigger demonstration.

Then, one day out of the blue, an email arrived confirming a positive DNA test for paternity. I had official proof I was your dad! As if we didn't already know that. The official test results still had to be sent to the consulate.

Thankfully, after all of the warnings we were given, we had completed the DNA testing in an unbelievably fast two weeks and five days. As soon as the hard copy was received by the U.S. consulate, the rest of the applications could be processed. There was possibly even more good news. At our consulate appointment, we had been told that it would take about three weeks to process your applications for passports. The consular officer also said, that in the case of dire circumstances, emergency passports could be generated in just around three *days*. I spoke to my parents, and we all agreed, with my dad's hospitalizations and worrisome outlook, along with the intensifying protests, we had all the emergency we needed. I sent an impassioned and sincere email to the consular officer expressing our qualification for emergency passport status, and to alert her that my official DNA test results were on their way.

The days continued to tick away as we cared for you and hoped for a speedy exit from the country. Three days after the consulate had received the test results, I picked up our emergency passports. The Consular Report of Birth Abroad would be mailed to us back in the U.S. I was so incredibly relieved and thankful! Just one week earlier, we couldn't tell if we would be leaving soon or stuck in Thailand another month.

We were going home!

Shortly before departure. Jeanie, Joseph, Dennis with Max and Alex.

Escaping Thailand

I woke up in the early morning, three days after picking up the emergency passports. After two long months in Bangkok, we would be leaving for America in hours. Incredibly, this was the day that our return flight had originally been scheduled! Ten weeks earlier, we had made a slightly educated guess as to when we would be able to fly home. We assumed that it would have to be amended. This is just one example of a number of things that happened to us that felt inexplicably perfect, despite all of the hardships we faced.

We had already packed most of our luggage a couple of days earlier. Of course, there was a pile of things we acquired during our stay that we just didn't have room or use for, such as a CD player and already outgrown preemie baby clothes. Everything useful, we offered to the apartment staff. They accepted, happily.

You boys were in for an amazing journey. The extent of your experience had been limited to several blocks around our apartment. That day you would be traveling thousands of miles to a different corner of the planet. If we had not been in a foreign country trying desperately to get home, flying with you babies, now, close to your original due date, would have seemed preposterous. Yet, it was time to get back to what we knew, and time to endure the inevitable hardship of travel required to get there.

I was looking down at both of you on the bed just before leaving. You were content and cooing, dressed in soft and white outfits Mom had picked out for you. You knew nothing of America. I found myself getting quite nostalgic about my homeland. There's nothing better to give you appreciation for something than being away from it. What little we had seen of Thailand was fascinating. But I love the United States. Alex and Max, you would grow up in the "land of the free, and the home of the brave", something very few people in the world could claim. It dawned on me that, despite my family being fully American for at least four generations, we had a big-time habit of birthing our kids overseas. For different reasons, seven of the recent births in our family had occurred outside of the U.S. My brothers and I were born in Guyana. My brother's daughters, adopted, had been born in China. And now, you, my sons, were born in Thailand. I think it's easy to forget the blessing we have as Americans. Perhaps those childbearing odysseys in my family have helped to keep our perspectives fresh.

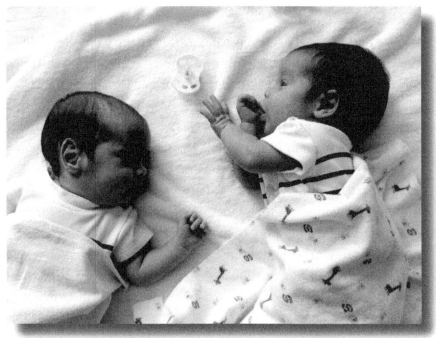

From left to right: Maximus and Alexander Hahle.

I was in my bedroom arranging suitcases when I heard the front door open. My mom started to scream like she was being attacked and in a struggle! We were just an hour from leaving time. I thought to myself, "My mom is being mugged! I'll run to her aid! I don't know if I can get there in time to save her!"

The front door was just 10 feet down the hall. It seemed to take me forever to get there as she yelled. I came around the corner to find my mother standing in the entryway alone. Apparently, when she had opened the door, a large cockroach was disturbed. It jumped out, scaring her and causing her to dance around as it scurried this way and that. The roach had quickly found its way under a step, and out of reach. That could have been a big problem for me. We were on our way out. Whoever was checking in next would have to wage that next battle.

We got into a taxi van. Suddenly, we were doing all the things we had done to get there in reverse. This time the infant car seats were filled. There was not an inch of space left in the jam-packed van. Thai law does not require the use of infant car seats. We didn't have any car seat bases to make them work properly anyway. So we held the car seats filled with you babies in our laps. Part of me wondered if we would be checking back into the apartment later that day after an unexpected obstruction at the airport. We had two newborn infants with us now. Their Thai birth mother was not present. Would the authorities let us pass? Only time would tell.

We checked our bags, and started the awkward movement through security. We passed a number of checkpoints, but at one in particular, the officer stopped me and looked on with suspicion. Somehow, Mom and Dad were processed first at a separate station, and got pushed on through without recognizing what had happened to you and me. The officer, who appeared to be in a bad mood, began asking questions, which I could barely understand. I showed him your passports and birth certificates.

"Where mother?" he barked.

"She is not traveling with us," I replied.

"Where mother??" he insisted.

I hesitated.

"She was a surrogate," I let out. I had been cautioned about using the word "surrogate," because of the locally, poorly-defined law and possible controversy it could spark, especially with the political protests escalating. What was I going to do, lie to this guy? I could have told him that she was ill, would be joining us later, or something else. I wouldn't feel right about it. I feared dishonesty could land us all in a lot more trouble. The officer looked on with an evil eye.

"Surrogate?" he uttered.

"Yes sir, surrogate." I confirmed and nodded. I was sweating. A line of people was forming behind me.

Where were Mom and Dad?? *This* was the scary moment we had been wondering about the whole time! And they had strolled off somewhere!

Then the officer barked something else, which I couldn't understand. He repeated himself with frustration, but I still couldn't get it. He motioned to a tiny camera at the front of his station. I realized he wanted to take a picture of me. I awkwardly stood in front of the camera with as much confidence and normalcy as I could muster. He clicked his computer mouse. Then he pointed at you, Alex, still in your car seat on the floor. In a moment, I got the gist of what he wanted and picked up the car seat. The officer gestured for me to position you in a particular spot and angle so that he could photograph your face. The line behind me grew longer.

Mom finally appeared around the corner. "Where did you go?" I asked her.

148

"We didn't know where you were!" She responded.

"Help me with this! He has to take pictures of them." We grabbed your car seat, Max, and raised it up the same way with the officer gesturing for the correct position.

After the pictures were taken and a few forms signed, he gestured to me to move on, like he was tired of dealing with me. Mom grabbed one of the car seats and we hurriedly made our way down the corridor. What a relief! I had been seeing visions of heading back into town alone with you boys – my parents missing.

We caught up with Dad who was surprised to see us. Apparently they had the impression that I had gotten through the station first. They had been trying to catch up to me.

Riding on a jumbo jet for 18 hours with carry-on luggage is an awkward task to begin with. Doing it all with two newborn infants who need diaper changes, feeding and who inevitably cry from time to time is a monumental feat.

We notified the airline in advance about you. They informed us that they could provide baby basinets that hook to a bulkhead right in front of our seats.

The first plane to Taipei only provided one basinet, which Max used. Alex spent most of his time in our arms or on a bed of blankets in an empty seat, which just happened to be in our row. At the end of this first flight, we waited

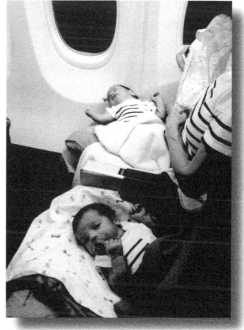

The first flight. Max at top. Alex at bottom.

149

until the plane was empty before moving. Many people passed by on their way out, stopping to admire you and say how cute you were.

The second flight, a 747, had plenty of room for two basinets. The hours were not easy. Luckily, the natural movement of the plane seemed to help calm you two, while the rumble of the engines helped to cloak any of your crying.

At long last, we touched down in Los Angeles. We had been gone so long that, in a way, it felt like another foreign country. My friend, David, and his son, Zack, had arrived to pick us up with two vehicles, complete with our infant car seat bases pre-installed. We sped away for the final leg of our journey home, which occurred without mishap.

The sun had set, and a cool mist was falling from the sky. As we arrived at my house and walked in with you boys, I felt time contract, as if I had never left. Bangkok felt like a strange dream. I had not slept at all on the long ride home, so I was in a nearly delirious state. Had we really gone to Thailand? Had I lived in a little apartment in another country for two months as I secured my newborn sons who returned with me? Maybe it was all in my head. Yet, still stuck in the car seats in front of me was the proof that it had all happened. Two little baby boys who had never been to Stagg Manor, were now here in the flesh, sleepily peeking out to see the living room and house they would grow up in.

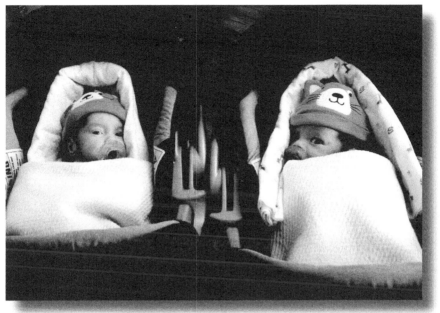

First moments in their new home. From left to right: Maximus and Alexander.

The Discomforts of Home

The next day, it was very, very hard to get up. We, especially Mom, had spent time during the night feeding and caring for you boys, as usual. So we were all still very drained. My good friend had stocked our refrigerator with all kinds of wonderful food, but that was one of our only comforts.

It was March third. The Christmas tree and decorations were still up! We had left in such a panic, we didn't have time to take them down. Worse, as we had noticed before going to bed, there was no running water! A neighbor clued us in that there had been a water main break at our curb. Apparently, the water had been flowing for three days before someone finally called and the city shut off the pressure. And *then*, we discovered that neither of our cars were starting. We had come six thousand miles for the comforts of home and landed in a place with more inconvenience than where we had been! Part of this was my own fault. I should have known to have my house sitter run the cars a little each week to keep them vital. But the water main? That was just horrible timing. Believe it or not, my house sitter had left town for a job opportunity just a week or so before the break.

In the face of all of these problems, I went out the front door for some fresh air and noticed something truly amazing. In the ficus tree at the walkway, about eye level from the ground, was a tiny little bird nest. Two, perfect, twin, hummingbird babies sat nestled against each other in this nest – their beaks pointing in opposite directions. My mind raced back to the egg I had found in the backyard, when the babies had been born, which had fallen from its tree. Once again, providence was mirroring my experience on the path to fatherhood. My sons were with us, and healthy. As I embraced that fact, the various tasks we faced around the house didn't seem quite so terrible.

Baby hummingbirds outside the house in North Hollywood, CA.

Within a couple weeks, things really were starting to feel right again. I was talking to my next-door neighbor, who is a cantankerous, 81-year old, about how things were going as a new father. He's always making little jokes about this thing or that – trying to catch me off guard. Looking for a funny reaction, he asked me if I was breast-feeding. "Ha ha," I replied. "Yeah right… No." Then I got serious. "But my mother is," I said with a perfectly straight face. His knees bent, and he looked up into my eyes with utter astonishment.

"Really?!?" he asked.

I couldn't hold my composure for long. With a heavy smirk on my face, I admitted what I had said was not true.

The Military Coup
and Crackdown

Six months after our return from Bangkok, political protests in
Thailand had continued to escalate. After a coup, the country
was under military control. I was told that there was a major
crackdown on surrogacy programs and IVF companies, resulting
in the shutdown of New Life Thailand, the very clinic I was
working with. This was not because the surrogacy programs and
clinics were doing anything necessarily wrong. I believe it was
simply because it was a practice that was not yet well defined in
Thai law and not properly regulated. Poorly overseen businesses
had the potential of exploiting Thai citizens (women). The
military leadership was trying to steady the country. This
seemed to be one industry that was being targeted for shutdown
until it was established more officially. Sadly, numerous families
were in the middle of their pregnancies, and it would be an even
harder process for them getting sorted out and back home with
their children than it was for us. This all sounded pretty scary.
Yet, I was encouraged to hear that the same branch of New Life
that was in Thailand, had been re-established in nearby Nepal.

Caring for Twins
as a Single Father

Alex and Max, we just celebrated your second birthday!

Max, you are now the slightly larger boy at 24.8 pounds, with Alex just behind at 23.7. I'm extremely relieved to be able to say that life has fully regained its normalcy. Oh, things are much different than they were before your birth! Yet everything seems manageable.

For the most part, everyone seems to get enough sleep. Each day since your birth has included little moments of joy as I hold you and am amazed that you are mine.

And you change *so* fast. You are constantly learning something new, and reminding me that you won't be toddlers for long. I can remember clearly the day that Alex put one hand out in front of the other, then his legs followed suit, and he crawled for the first time.

Max, you didn't crawl first. You were the first to stand, and the first baby to get a tooth. These moments of literally leaping forward have made each day a new adventure. I am so looking forward to real conversations with you.

There have also been inevitable problems and accidents. I was back at work editing one evening when I received a phone call from my father. Alex, you had been taken to the emergency room after pulling a fresh, hot cup of coffee off the kitchen counter straight onto you. I was told that the resulting burns covered half of your face. I raced to the ER not knowing how bad the situation really was. Thankfully, within a couple of weeks, the burned skin flaked off, and you were not permanently scarred. This is just one example of numerous challenges we have faced over the months that could not be predicted.

Raising the two of you together, as a single parent, has been, as anyone would expect, an enormous undertaking. It's hard for me to see how I would cope without your able-bodied, retired grandparents living in the house with me, taking on huge childcare responsibilities. I can't give them enough praise for the gift they have given, both in Thailand and back at home. It has taken the team of three of us adults, plus the occasional babysitter, to care properly for you twins.

My parents are my heroes. You boys will grow up knowing how important they have been to us all, and how much they love us. My hat is off to all of the single parents out there who are not rich or blessed with advantageous circumstances, who find a way to raise their babies. May God bless them indeed.

A good friend of mine has told me, half joking, that I need to start early instilling in you boys that, when I get old, it is your duty to take extra good care of me. That is most certainly true. Yet every time I think of his advice, I am reminded of my own parents, and how it is particularly important that I make good with them in the years to come. I intend to do just that.

Looking back at my journey to become a parent, I see quite a struggle. I'm proud of what I achieved. It was an amazing number of hoops to jump through. Just a few years before your births, I considered the amount of money involved and it didn't seem quite reachable. None of it would have been possible without the undeniable determination I had to succeed. And I would say *that* determination came from love that I was ready to give to you. It is apparent to me that much of what I had been doing in the years leading up to your birth was "nesting." I think

I had been preparing for you unconsciously in various ways ever since I was a child myself.

I look at other people with children today and sometimes forget that most of them didn't have to go through what I did to have kids. They don't even know how lucky they are. For them, having a child was as easy and free as doing what came naturally. Of course, I don't resent them. And their children are miracles. For the rest of us, parenthood is a distinction that has to be earned with blood, sweat, and tears. And I would earn it all over again for you boys.

Alexander and Maximus, you are the most wonderful realization of my dream to become a parent that I could have possibly imagined. I am so very proud to be your father. Your whole lives are ahead of you. I want nothing more for you than the fulfillment of your own dreams. Make use of every opportunity you have in this life to live. Help and love as many people as you can along the way. And always, always remember how much I love you.

Acknowledgments

David Garber

Hava Garber

Chris Neely

Jeanie Hahle

Dennis Hahle

Carole Mathison

Elma Jean Beatty

Tom Profit

Andrew Hubrechsen-Yung

Paul Hubrechsen-Yung

Berry Gentry